W9-AOO-236

LOW-FAT
VEGETARIAN COOKING

LOW-FAT VEGETARIAN COOKING

Innovative Vegetarian Recipes for the Adventurous Cook

JENNY STACEY

Eagle Editions

A QUANTUM BOOK

Published by Eagle Editions Ltd.
11 Heathfield
Royston
Hertfordshire SG8 5BW

Copyright ©MCMXCVII
Quintet Publishing Ltd.

This edition printed 2004

All rights reserved.
This book is protected by copyright. No
part of it may be reproduced, stored in a
retrieval system, or transmitted in any form
or by any means, without the prior
permission in writing of the Publisher, nor
be otherwise circulated in any form of
binding or cover other than that in which it
is published and without a similar condition
including this condition being imposed on
the subsequent publisher.

ISBN 1-86160-991-4

QUMLVC

This book is produced by
Quantum Publishing Ltd
6 Blundell Street
London N7 9BH

Printed in Singapore by
Star Standard Industries (Pte) Ltd

CONTENTS

INTRODUCTION

Low in fat does not have to mean lacking in flavour or in quality. There are many foods that you can eat without feeling guilty that you are eating too much fat. Low fat simply requires you to change some cooking methods, use alternative ingredients, and to understand a few fundamental points. Once you have grasped the basic principles, they can be quickly adapted to all of your favourite dishes to open up a whole new world of fun, healthy food.

We consume far too much fat in our daily diet in one form or another. Most of the fat is usually hidden in items such as biscuits, cakes, creamy sauces, cooked meat, processed foods, and fast foods. The problem is many of us do not understand fats. We remember the words "saturated", "monounsaturated", and "polyunsaturated", being mentioned, but do we really know what difference they make to our waistlines and well-being?

What are the different kinds of fat?

Most of us have been brought up on a diet containing high-fat foods such as meat, dairy products and fast, convenient foods. To follow a low-fat diet we must first cut down on the amount of fat that we eat and learn to use foods with a lower saturated fat content. But how do we know what type of fat we are eating in order to make educated choices? Where are the saturated fats found?

Saturated fats are generally solid at room temperature. It is these fats that tend to raise blood cholesterol levels. They are usually found in animal products such as butter, lard, suet and meat. Two vegetable oils also contain saturated fats. These are labelled as coconut oil and palm oil.

Unsaturated fats known as *monounsaturated* or *polyunsaturated* are liquid at room temperature, and do not appear to promote increases in blood cholesterol. Mono-unsaturated fats are known to have a neutral effect and are found in oils such as groundnut oil and olive oil. Polyunsaturated fats have been found to actually lower blood cholesterol. These fats are found in oils such as corn oil, soy oil, safflower oil, walnut and sesame oils.

The term "cholesterol" has been prominent in the headlines in recent years, giving us yet another number to confuse and worry about. In fact, we do need a certain amount of cholesterol in our bodies because it is vital for human tissues and cells and for making hormones. This is not an invitation to eat. We produce a certain amount of cholesterol in our liver. It is this cholesterol that usually is used for our body's necessary functions. Therefore, when dietary cholesterol is consumed in excess our body can no longer absorb it for constructive use and it then finds its way to the blood vessels where excess build-up can lead to atherosclerosis (a disease state in which fatty substances, mainly cholesterol, slowly accumulate on the lining of artery walls). Slow continuous progression of this disease state can result in a leading cause of death, a heart attack.

It is possible to do something about this situation. Cutting out high-fat, processed food or added fat will bring daily fat intake down. Simply begin to reduce the quantity of cholesterol-rich foods you eat and your cholesterol count will begin to reduce. According to a study conducted in the USA in 1983 on 3,806 men, when drug therapy and dietary treatment were implemented on men at high risk for heart disease, a 1 per cent fall in cholesterol produced a 2 per cent drop in the rate of coronary heart disease.

Foods high in cholesterol which should generally be avoided include egg yolks, offal, lard, animal fats and dairy products, such as high-fat cheeses, hard cheeses, cream, butter and whole milk.

Polyunsaturated fats are found in oils such as olive, safflower, walnut and sesame.

Low fat or no fat?

Although it is recommended that fat intakes are severely reduced, everything in moderation is the best motto. No-one is suggesting a totally fat-free diet. We require a certain amount of fat for bodily functions, such as producing linoleic acid for skin maintenance, growth in children, and for the supply of compounds vital for our bodies to function. As we cannot produce these compounds it is essential we obtain them from food. Besides these functions, fat also enhances the flavour of food and to cut it out altogether is not recommended. It is suggested that 25–30 per cent of our total calories in any one day should come from fat, although this figure is considered too high by some experts.

Less than 10 per cent of our daily calories should come from saturated fats, up to 10 per cent may come from polyunsaturated fats and the remainder of our intake may come from monounsaturated sources. At present the majority of the population obtains at least 40 per cent of their calories from fat, so there is plenty of room for improvement.

Eating a low-fat diet is not just another fad; it will actually improve your life and could extend life expectancy. It could also mean you can enjoy every moment you cook and eat without bearing the guilt which accompanies a high-fat meal. There has been a great deal of medical and scientific research over the years which shows that the diet eaten by modern society is a major cause of disease. The saying "you are what you eat" has never been truer. Nearly two-thirds of the population will suffer stroke, heart attack or a form of cancer as a direct result of what they eat. The problem begins in childhood and sets a pattern for later life. Fortunately, heart disease is a slow process which gives us time to arrest and correct the situation. It has been proven that people who change to a low-fat diet reduce their risk of heart disease. High-fat diets are associated with other diseases such as gallstones, diabetes, obesity, stomach upsets, thrombosis, eczema, asthma, arthritis and general lethargy. Reducing your fat intake can substantially reduce the risk of these diseases. A low-fat diet will not only make you feel better and have more energy, but will also make you look better.

How to change your diet

Talk is cheap. Action speaks louder than words. Now that you know the reasons why you should reduce your fat intake, let's discuss how.

● Cut away visible fats in your diet, such as those used in cooking and those eaten as snacks.
● Eliminate high-fat potato crisps, biscuits, fried foods, sweets and processed foods. Substitute fat-free/low-fat crisps, pretzels and fat-free biscuits.
● Reduce the amount of hard cheeses used. Most of them contain 30–40 per cent fat in relation to weight. It is better to use a little strong-flavoured cheese than a lot of mild cheese whether in cooking or in sandwiches.
● Limit egg yolks to three a week, but continue to use the egg whites as often as desired.
● Begin to discover the aroma and flavour of fresh herbs, which used wisely can enhance your cooking a great deal.

Beans and pulses are high vitality, high fibre foods. Experts agree a healthy diet is one which is high in fibre, low in fat.

Chopped fresh herbs make excellent flavouring and the best way to appreciate them is freshly picked.

● Avoid fried foods. Use other cooking methods such as grilling, sautéeing and steaming. Poaching in stock or vegetable juice using herbs and spices is an alternative.

● When making stews, casseroles and soups, leave enough time to cool then skim the fat from the top before serving. You'll be amazed how much fat you will save.

● Add more grains, pulses and beans to your diet. With the wide variety now available on the market it is easy to produce delicious dishes while reducing your fat intake. Beans are high in protein, high in fibre and low in fat.

● Increase your variety of pasta intake which is filling, healthy and low in fat. Remember, the pasta itself is not fattening but what you may put on top of it.

● Switch to skimmed milk. You will hardly notice the difference. In recipes calling for cream, use whole milk or yogurt; for whipping cream, use chilled evaporated skimmed milk.

● Eat more soups, salads and fresh vegetables, which are cheaper and healthier than packaged foods.

● In cooking, substitute curd cheeses for cream cheese.

● In recipes calling for soured cream substitute yogurt. To keep yogurt from separating in foods to be cooked, first mix 1 tablespoon cornflour with 1 tablespoon of yogurt and stir into rest of yogurt, then into your recipe.

● Use non-stick pans where possible and always use a lid. If oil is required, brush the pan lightly with a small amount rather than pouring in a pool of it. Cook onions and vegetables in a little stock in place of sautéeing in oil.

● Alcohol is allowed in moderation and can actually change the way your body reacts to cholesterol. One or two servings of alcohol a day can be very beneficial according to recent studies, but it should not be consumed in large quantities.

Understanding labels and tables

A proper low-fat diet begins in the supermarket. It is important that you feel comfortable with the selections that you will be purchasing for you and your family. Understanding food labelling and marketing is the number one strategy in becoming a successful shopper.

Food labels must give specific information so that you can make informed choices between foods. The law controls the label information to protect you from false claims or misleading descriptions as well as helping you to meet your healthy eating goals. There are several legal requirements for food package labelling including the name or description of the food, an ingredient list (in descending order of weight), some form of date marking and instruction for safe storage, a weight, volume or number in the pack, the name and address of the manufacturer, packer or retailer and any preparation or cooking instructions.

Food companies do not, by law, have to give information on the label about the energy and nutrients in the food, though the vast majority do give this information.

European Community law requires that when nutrition information is given it must be given in one or two ways. A company can label only the energy (kJ or kcal), protein, carbohydrate and fat content. Alternatively, in addition it can include how much of the carbohydration are sugars, the amount of saturates in the fat and the amounts of fibre and sodium. Further information such as the amount of polyunsaturates in the fat or the quantity of a range of vitamins and minerals may also be added. Information must be given per 100g or 100ml. Some companies give information per serving or portion as well.

Supermarket chains sets their own criteria for nutritional claims and often use labels or symbols to identify foods which are for instance "low fat". These are a quick guide but may mean something different on each food.

Guidelines issued for nutritional claims pertaining to fat, saturates and sodium are as follows: "fat free" means that there is less than 0.15g per 100g, "low fat" that there is less than 6g per 100g and "reduced fat" that it contains 25 per cent or less. "Saturate free" means less than 0.1g per 100g, "low in saturates" less than 3g per 100g and "reduced" that it contains 25 per cent or less.

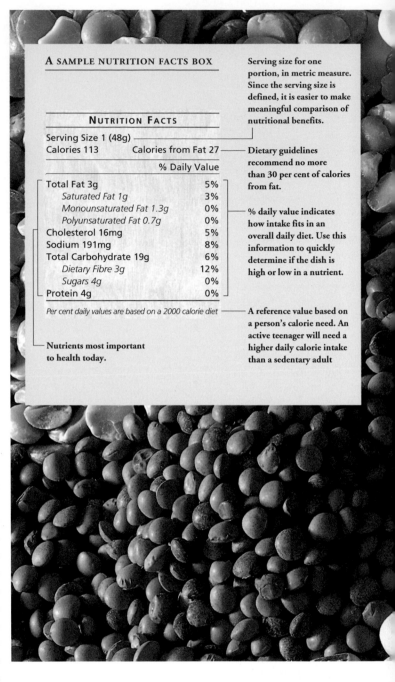

A SAMPLE NUTRITION FACTS BOX		Serving size for one portion, in metric measure. Since the serving size is defined, it is easier to make meaningful comparison of nutritional benefits.

NUTRITION FACTS

Serving Size 1 (48g)
Calories 113 — Calories from Fat 27

	% Daily Value
Total Fat 3g	5%
Saturated Fat 1g	3%
Monounsaturated Fat 1.3g	0%
Polyunsaturated Fat 0.7g	0%
Cholesterol 16mg	5%
Sodium 191mg	8%
Total Carbohydrate 19g	6%
Dietary Fibre 3g	12%
Sugars 4g	0%
Protein 4g	0%

Per cent daily values are based on a 2000 calorie diet

Dietary guidelines recommend no more than 30 per cent of calories from fat.

% daily value indicates how intake fits in an overall daily diet. Use this information to quickly determine if the dish is high or low in a nutrient.

A reference value based on a person's calorie need. An active teenager will need a higher daily calorie intake than a sedentary adult

Nutrients most important to health today.

If it is claimed a food is "sodium free" it should contain less than 5mg per 100g, if "low in sodium" it should contain 40mg or less per 100g, "reduced sodium" foods should contain 25 per cent or less and "no added sodium" must apply to both the food and any of its ingredients.

The labels giving such nutritional information will allow you to compare ingredients or products of similar foods and allow you to make the choice of purchasing a lower fat or lower calorie food.

Increase your variety of delicious dishes by using pulses such as lentils, black-eyed peas and kidney beans.

There is a nutritional analysis of each of the recipes in this book to help you understand what you are eating and to plan your meals accordingly. The facts and information provided by this book are based upon the most recent scientific knowledge as of 1996. The nutritional analyses are a close estimation but not an exact science since various sources provide different nutritional analysis of specific food items. Remember, it is not imperative that each recipe provides under 25–30 per cent of its calories as fat but rather that of the whole day. It may be unrealistic for certain recipes to be under 5g of fat per serving, especially a main entrée, but coupled with a low-fat appetizer and a low-fat vegetable dish you should be on your way to a healthier lifestyle.

BRIGHT BREAKFASTS

Apricot Yogurt Crunch

Banana Energy

Crunchy Morning Scones

Grilled Pink Grapefruit

Porridge with Poached Fruit

Breakfast Hash

Fruit Kebabs

Hash Brown Potatoes with Baked Beans

Bread Pudding

Breakfast Muffins

Strawberry Cocktail

Apple Drop Scones

Spiced Pears

Spicy Fruit Salad

APRICOT YOGURT CRUNCH

SERVES 4

A variation on a Scottish dish, the crunchy porridge oats, spicy yogurt, and lightly poached fruit make an attractive morning dish.

275 g (10 oz) apricots, pitted

45 ml (3 tbsp) honey

50 g (2 oz) porridge oats, toasted

2.5–5 g (½–1 tsp) ground ginger

275 g (10 oz) low-fat natural yogurt

≈ Place the apricots in a pan with 150 ml (¼ pint) water and 15 ml (1 tablespoon) of the honey. Cook for 5 minutes until softened and drain.

≈ Mix the oats and remaining honey in a bowl. Stir the ginger into the yogurt.

≈ Alternately layer the fruit, yogurt and oat mixtures into serving glasses. Chill and serve.

NUTRITION FACTS	
Serving Size 1 (162g)	
Calories 140	Calories from Fat 18
	% Daily Value
Total Fat 2g	2%
Saturated Fat 1g	4%
Monounsaturated Fat 0.5g	0%
Polyunsaturated Fat 0.2g	0%
Cholesterol 4mg	1%
Sodium 78mg	3%
Total Carbohydrate 28g	9%
Dietary Fibre 2g	7%
Sugars 23g	0%
Protein 5g	0%

Per cent daily values are based on a 2000 calorie diet

BANANA ENERGY

SERVES 4

If you can't face a full breakfast in the morning, take your energy in a glass with this nutritious drink.

4 large bananas, peeled and cut into chunks

15 ml (1 tbsp) lemon juice

300 ml (½ pint) low-fat natural yogurt

300 ml (½ pint) skimmed milk

30 ml (2 tbsp) honey

lemon slices and mint sprigs, for garnish

≈ Place all the ingredients in a food processor or blender. Liquidize for 1 minute until smooth. Pour into tall serving glasses, garnish, and serve immediately.

NUTRITION FACTS	
Serving Size 1 (276g)	
Calories 210	Calories from Fat 18
	% Daily Value
Total Fat 2g	3%
Saturated Fat 1g	5%
Monounsaturated Fat 0.3g	0%
Polyunsaturated Fat 0.1g	0%
Cholesterol 6mg	2%
Sodium 91mg	4%
Total Carbohydrate 44g	15%
Dietary Fibre 3g	11%
Sugars 34g	0%
Protein 8g	0%

Per cent daily values are based on a 2000 calorie diet

Apricot Yogurt Crunch ▶

CRUNCHY MORNING SCONES

MAKES 14

These lightly spiced scones are delicious served piping hot with cinnamon yogurt, thus eliminating the necessity for butter.

115 g (4 oz) self-raising flour

115 g (4 oz) wholemeal self-raising flour

pinch of ground cinnamon

pinch of ground nutmeg

25 g (1 oz) polyunsaturated margarine

50 g (2 oz) all-bran cereal

15 g (1 tbsp) chopped, skinned hazelnuts

45 g (3 tbsp) sultanas

1 egg

90 ml (6 tbsp) skimmed milk

For the cinnamon yogurt

150 ml (¼ pint) low-fat natural yogurt

1.5 g (¼ tsp) ground cinnamon

2.5 ml (½ tsp) honey

NUTRITION FACTS	
Serving Size 1 (48g)	
Calories 113	Calories from Fat 27
	% Daily Value
Total Fat 3g	5%
Saturated Fat 1g	3%
Monounsaturated Fat 1.3g	0%
Polyunsaturated Fat 0.7g	0%
Cholesterol 16mg	5%
Sodium 191mg	8%
Total Carbohydrate 19g	6%
Dietary Fibre 3g	12%
Sugars 4g	0%
Protein 4g	0%

Per cent daily values are based on a 2000 calorie diet

≈ Preheat the oven to 200°C (400°F, Gas 6). Place the flours and spices in a bowl and rub in the margarine to resemble fine breadcrumbs. Stir in the all-bran, nuts and sultanas. Stir in the egg and milk and bring together to form a soft dough.

≈ Knead the dough on a lightly floured surface and cut into eight 7.5 cm (3 in) rounds with a cutter. Brush the tops with a little extra milk and place on a floured baking sheet. Bake for 20 minutes until risen and golden. Mix together the yogurt ingredients and serve with the warm scones. Sprinkle with extra cinnamon to garnish, if desired.

GRILLED PINK GRAPEFRUIT

SERVES 4

A quick, simple breakfast; it may be speedy but its flavour is sensational.

2 Florida pink grapefruit
30 ml (2 tbsp) honey
pinch of ground allspice
mint sprigs to garnish (optional)

≈ Cut the skin away from the grapefruit, remove any remaining pith and cut each grapefruit into quarters. Place the quarters in a heatproof shallow dish.

≈ Mix together the honey and allspice and spoon over the grapefruit pieces. Cook under the grill for 5 minutes. Serve garnished with mint if desired.

NUTRITION FACTS	
Serving Size 1 (134g)	
Calories 69	Calories from Fat 0
	% Daily Value
Total Fat 0g	0%
Saturated Fat 0g	0%
Monounsaturated Fat 0.0g	0%
Polyunsaturated Fat 0.0g	0%
Cholesterol 0mg	0%
Sodium 1mg	0%
Total Carbohydrate 18g	6%
Dietary Fibre 1g	6%
Sugars 16g	0%
Protein 1g	0%

Per cent daily values are based on a 2000 calorie diet

PORRIDGE WITH POACHED FRUIT

SERVES 4

A quick porridge which can be made in advance or the night before. Hearty and filling, the poached fruit sets it off perfectly.

175 g (6 oz) porridge oats

1.05 litres (1¾ pints) skimmed milk

175 g (6 oz) plums, halved, pitted and sliced

120 ml (8 tbsp) honey

≈ Place the porridge oats in a pan with the milk. Bring to the boil, reduce the heat and simmer for 5 minutes, stirring until thickened.

≈ Meanwhile, place the plums in a saucepan with 30 ml (2 tablespoons) of honey and 150 ml (¼ pint) water. Bring to the boil, reduce heat and simmer for 5 minutes until softened. Drain well.

≈ Spoon the porridge into individual bowls and top with the poached plums. Serve hot with the remaining 90 ml (6 tablespoons) of honey.

NUTRITION FACTS	
Serving Size 1 (359g)	
Calories 310	Calories from Fat 18
	% Daily Value
Total Fat 2g	2%
Saturated Fat 1g	7%
Monounsaturated Fat 0.3g	0%
Polyunsaturated Fat 0.3g	0%
Cholesterol 5mg	2%
Sodium 183mg	8%
Total Carbohydrate 66g	22%
Dietary Fibre 2g	7%
Sugars 46g	0%
Protein 11g	0%

Per cent daily values are based on a 2000 calorie diet

BREAKFAST HASH

MAKES 4

For a speedier breakfast, cook the potatoes for this tasty dish the evening before and store in a sealed bag in the refrigerator until required.

675 g (1½ lbs) peeled, cubed potatoes

15 ml (1 tbsp) sunflower oil

1 red pepper, seeded and halved

1 green pepper, seeded and halved

2 tomatoes, diced

115 g (4 oz) open cap mushrooms, peeled, quartered

30 g (2 tbsp) fresh chopped parsley

ground black pepper

≈ Cook the potatoes in boiling water for 7 minutes, drain well. Heat the sunflower oil in a large frying pan, add the potatoes and cook for 10 minutes, stirring.

≈ Chop the red and green peppers and add to the pan with the tomatoes and mushrooms. Cook for 5 minutes, stirring constantly, add the chopped parsley, season to taste and serve.

NUTRITION FACTS	
Serving Size 1 (277g)	
Calories 179	Calories from Fat 36
	% Daily Value
Total Fat 4g	6%
Saturated Fat 0g	2%
Monounsaturated Fat 1.6g	0%
Polyunsaturated Fat 1.6g	0%
Cholesterol 0mg	0%
Sodium 88mg	4%
Total Carbohydrate 34g	11%
Dietary Fibre 4g	15%
Sugars 6g	0%
Protein 4g	0%

Per cent daily values are based on a 2000 calorie diet

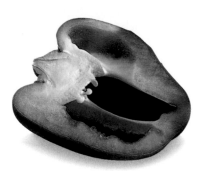

Breakfast Hash ▶

FRUIT KEBABS

SERVES 4

The perfect way to present fresh fruit, these lightly grilled kebabs with a hint of mint make a refreshing start to the day.

30 g (2 tbsp) caster sugar

2 mint sprigs, plus extra for garnish

1 papaya, halved, seeded and
    chopped into 5 cm (2 in) squares

1 mango, stoned and chopped into
    5 cm (2 in) squares

1 star fruit, sliced

2 kiwi fruit, thickly sliced

≈ Soak four wooden skewers in water for 30 minutes. Remove when ready to use. Place the sugar, mint and 150 ml (¼ pint) water in a pan. Heat gently to dissolve the sugar and then bring to the boil until reduced by half. Discard the mint.

≈ Thread the fruit onto the skewers, alternating the varieties. Brush with the syrup and grill for 10 minutes, turning and brushing until heated through. Serve hot, garnished with mint.

HASH BROWN POTATOES WITH BAKED BEANS

SERVES 6

These golden potato cakes are served with a spicy bean dish, and are perfect for mopping up the delicious juices. Make the bean dish in advance and keep in the refrigerator until morning. Simply heat the beans in a pan over a gentle heat.

≈ Drain the soaked beans and rinse well under cold water. Drain and put in a large saucepan with 475 ml (16 fl oz) of water. Bring the beans to the boil and boil rapidly for 10 minutes. Reduce the heat to a simmer, cover and cook for 1 hour or until the beans are cooked, topping up the water if necessary. Drain the beans and return them to the pan. Stir in the vegetable stock, dried mustard, onion, molasses, tomatoes, tomato purée and basil. Season well and cook for 15 minutes or until the vegetables have cooked.

≈ Meanwhile, make the potato cakes while the beans are cooking. Cook the potatoes in boiling water for 20 minutes or until soft. Drain well and mash with the milk.

≈ Add the onion and garlic, mixing well and form into twelve equal-sized cakes. Brush a non-stick frying pan with the oil and warm over a medium heat. Cook the potato cakes for 15–20 minutes, turning once until golden brown. Serve hot with the baked beans.

NUTRITION FACTS	
Serving Size 1 (260g)	
Calories 154	Calories from Fat 9
	% Daily Value
Total Fat 1g	1%
Saturated Fat 0g	0%
Monounsaturated Fat 0.0g	0%
Polyunsaturated Fat 0.2g	0%
Cholesterol 0mg	0%
Sodium 12mg	0%
Total Carbohydrate 37g	12%
Dietary Fibre 6g	23%
Sugars 25g	0%
Protein 1g	0%

Per cent daily values are based on a 2000 calorie diet

For the baked beans

225 g (8 oz) dried navy beans,
  soaked overnight

150 ml (¼ pint) vegetable stock

2.5 g (½ tsp) dried mustard

1 onion, chopped

30 ml (2 tbsp) dark molasses

225 g (8 oz) tomatoes, peeled,
  chopped

15 ml (1 tbsp) tomato purée

15 g (1 tbsp) fresh chopped basil

ground black pepper

For the potato cakes

675 g (1½ lbs) peeled, cubed
  potatoes

30 ml (2 tbsp) skimmed milk

1 onion, chopped

1 garlic clove, crushed

10 ml (2 tsp) sunflower oil

Hash Brown Potatoes with Baked Beans

NUTRITION FACTS	
Serving Size 1 (194g)	
Calories 241	Calories from Fat 18
	% Daily Value
Total Fat 2g	4%
Saturated Fat 0g	2%
Monounsaturated Fat 0.7g	0%
Polyunsaturated Fat 0.9g	0%
Cholesterol 0mg	0%
Sodium 125mg	5%
Total Carbohydrate 46g	15%
Dietary Fibre 8g	30%
Sugars 2g	0%
Protein 11g	0%

Per cent daily values are based on a 2000 calorie diet

BREAD PUDDING

SERVES 8

Renowned as a delicious, but fattening dish, this savoury bread pudding is the perfect example of adapting a recipe to low-fat without compromising on taste.

≈ Spread the bread with the margarine and cut each slice into four triangles by cutting on the diagonal.

≈ Place the peppers skin side uppermost on a rack and grill for 10 minutes until blackened. Place in a plastic bag with tongs, seal and let cool. Peel off the the skins and discard. Slice the peppers into thin strips.

≈ Layer the bread, peppers, tomatoes and half of the cheese in a large shallow ovenproof dish. Mix the egg white and milk together and pour over the bread. Allow to stand for 30 minutes.

≈ Sprinkle the remaining cheese over the dish and season. Cook in the oven at 170°C (325°F, Gas 3) for 45 minutes until set and risen. Serve hot.

6 slices wholemeal bread, with crusts
   removed
15 g (1 tbsp) polyunsaturated
   margarine
1 red pepper, halved and seeded
1 green pepper, halved and seeded
2 tomatoes, chopped
50 g (2 oz) low-fat Cheddar cheese,
   grated
2 egg whites, beaten
475 ml (16 fl oz) skimmed milk
ground black pepper

NUTRITION FACTS

Serving Size 1 (165g)

Calories 112	Calories from Fat 18
	% Daily Value
Total Fat 2g	**4%**
Saturated Fat 1g	*3%*
Monounsaturated Fat 1.0g	*0%*
Polyunsaturated Fat 0.7g	*0%*
Cholesterol 1mg	**0%**
Sodium 214mg	**9%**
Total Carbohydrate 16g	**5%**
Dietary Fibre 2g	*9%*
Sugars 5g	*0%*
Protein 8g	**0%**

Per cent daily values are based on a 2000 calorie diet

BREAKFAST MUFFINS

MAKES 12

Breakfast wouldn't be breakfast without muffins. This healthy version gives you all the goodness you'd want from an old favourite.

≈ Place the flours, baking powder, muesli, dates and brown sugar in a bowl. In a separate bowl, mix together the egg white, milk, and margarine. Add to the dry ingredients all at once. Stir gently.

≈ Spoon the mixture into eight muffin cases to two-thirds full. Bake in the oven at 220°C (425°F, Gas 7) for 20–25 minutes until risen and golden. Serve warm.

75 g (3 oz) wholemeal flour
115 g (4 oz) plain flour
15 g (1 tbsp) baking powder
65 g (2½ oz) muesli
30 ml (2 tbsp) chopped dates
10 g (2 tsp) soft brown sugar
1 egg white, whisked
150 ml (¼ pint) skimmed milk
30 g (2 tbsp) polyunsaturated
   margarine, melted

NUTRITION FACTS

Serving Size 1 (46g)

Calories 119	Calories from Fat 27
	% Daily Value
Total Fat 3g	**4%**
Saturated Fat 1g	*3%*
Monounsaturated Fat 0.9g	*0%*
Polyunsaturated Fat 0.7g	*0%*
Cholesterol 0mg	**0%**
Sodium 170mg	**7%**
Total Carbohydrate 21g	**7%**
Dietary Fibre 1g	*5%*
Sugars 5g	*0%*
Protein 3g	**0%**

Per cent daily values are based on a 2000 calorie diet

Bread Pudding ▶

225 g (8 oz) strawberries, hulled and chopped

150 ml (¼ pint) cranberry juice

30 ml (2 tbsp) honey

2.5 g (½ tsp) ground ginger

475 ml (16 fl oz) sparkling mineral water

ice and mint sprigs to serve

4 whole strawberries, for garnish

NUTRITION FACTS

Serving Size 1 (265g)

Calories 85	Calories from Fat 0
	% Daily Value

Total Fat 0g	0%
Saturated Fat 0g	0%
Monounsaturated Fat 0.0g	0%
Polyunsaturated Fat 0.2g	0%
Cholesterol 0mg	0%
Sodium 3mg	0%
Total Carbohydrate 21g	7%
Dietary Fibre 2g	9%
Sugars 20g	0%
Protein 1g	0%

Per cent daily values are based on a 2000 calorie diet

For the scones

50 g (2 oz) wholemeal flour

5 g (1 tsp) baking powder

5 g (1 tsp) caster sugar

1 medium egg, beaten

85 ml (2½ fl oz) skimmed milk

1 green dessert apple, cored and chopped

15 g (1 tbsp) raisins

For the yogurt sauce

150 ml (1¼ pints) low-fat natural yogurt

2.5 g (½ tsp) ground cinnamon

5 ml (1 tsp) honey

NUTRITION FACTS

Serving Size 1 (122g)

Calories 131	Calories from Fat 18
	% Daily Value

Total Fat 2g	3%
Saturated Fat 1g	4%
Monounsaturated Fat 0.7g	0%
Polyunsaturated Fat 0.3g	0%
Cholesterol 55mg	18%
Sodium 368mg	15%
Total Carbohydrate 23g	8%
Dietary Fibre 3g	10%
Sugars 11g	0%
Protein 6g	0%

Per cent daily values are based on a 2000 calorie diet

STRAWBERRY COCKTAIL

SERVES 4

A refreshing breakfast cocktail with a sparkle. It is as quick and easy to make as it is to drink.

≈ Place the strawberries, cranberry juice, honey and ginger in a food processor and blend for 30 seconds until smooth.

≈ Add the sparkling mineral water, ice and mint. Pour into glasses, garnish, and serve immediately.

APPLE DROP SCONES

SERVES 4

This healthy version of a breakfast favourite is filled with chunks of crisp apple which are complemented by the cinnamon spiced yogurt sauce.

≈ Sift the flour and baking powder for the scones into a mixing bowl and stir in the sugar. Make a well in the centre and beat in the egg and milk to make a smooth batter. Stir in the apple and raisins, mixing well.

≈ Brush a heavy based non-stick frying pan with a little oil and warm over medium heat. Divide the batter into eight equal portions and drop four portions into the pan, spacing them well apart. Cook for 2–3 minutes until the top of each drop scone begins to bubble. Turn the scones over and cook for 1 minute. Transfer to a warmed plate and keep hot while cooking the remaining four scones.

≈ Mix the yogurt sauce ingredients together in a bowl and serve with the hot drop scones.

Apple Drop Scones ▶

SPICED PEARS

SERVES 4

The aroma from this dish is almost as good as the taste, and all part of the enjoyment. If liked, serve with a spoonful of natural yogurt or cottage cheese.

≈ Place the pear halves in a pan with the fruit juice, spices, raisins and sugar. Heat gently to dissolve the sugar and then bring to the boil.

≈ Reduce the heat to a simmer and cook for a further 10 minutes until the pears are softened. Serve hot with the syrup.

4 large ripe pears, peeled, halved and cored

300 ml (½ pint) mango juice

1 cinnamon stick, crushed

2.5 g (½ tsp) grated nutmeg

45 g (3 tbsp) raisins

30 g (2 tbsp) soft brown sugar

NUTRITION FACTS	
Serving Size 1 (259g)	
Calories 204	Calories from Fat 18
	% Daily Value
Total Fat 2g	3%
Saturated Fat 0g	0%
Monounsaturated Fat 0.1g	0%
Polyunsaturated Fat 0.2g	0%
Cholesterol 0mg	0%
Sodium 21mg	1%
Total Carbohydrate 50g	17%
Dietary Fibre 7g	27%
Sugars 37g	0%
Protein 1g	0%

Per cent daily values are based on a 2000 calorie diet

SPICY FRUIT SALAD

SERVES 4

Dried fruits are filled with goodness and have a delicious, concentrated flavour of their own. With many varieties now available it is easy to mix delicious combinations to create your personal favourite fruit salad.

≈ Place the fruits in a bowl and add the cinnamon and orange juice. Cover and leave to soak overnight.

≈ Place the contents of the bowl in a saucepan with the mint and bring to the boil, reduce the heat to a simmer and cook for 20 minutes until the fruits have softened. Cool and transfer to the refrigerator. Cover until required.

≈ Remove the mint from the salad. Mix together the yogurt and orange zest. Serve with the fruit salad.

115 g (4 oz) dried apricots

50 g (2 oz) dried peaches

50 g (2 oz) dried mango

50 g (2 oz) dried pears

115 g (4 oz) dried stoned prunes

5 g (1 tsp) ground cinnamon

900 ml (1½ pints) orange juice

3 mint sprigs

150 ml (¼ pint) low-fat natural yogurt

grated zest of 1 orange

NUTRITION FACTS	
Serving Size 1 (370g)	
Calories 368	Calories from Fat 18
	% Daily Value
Total Fat 2g	3%
Saturated Fat 0g	2%
Monounsaturated Fat 0.5g	0%
Polyunsaturated Fat 0.3g	0%
Cholesterol 2mg	1%
Sodium 36mg	2%
Total Carbohydrate 83g	30%
Dietary Fibre 8g	31%
Sugars 70g	0%
Protein 6g	0%

Per cent daily values are based on a 2000 calorie diet

Spiced Pears ▶

SIMPLE APPETIZERS AND HOT SOUPS

Cruditées with Chilli Tomato Dip

Baked Potato Skins

Vegetable Kebabs

Vegetable Enchiladas

Vegetable and Bean Soup

Vegetable Jambalaya

Courgette and Mint Soup

Chicory and Orange Salad

Spinach Pâté

Mediterranean Toasts

Mixed Bean and Vegetable Salad

Corn Chowder

Marinated Mushrooms

Asparagus with Red Pepper Sauce

Mediterranean Salad

Pumpkin Soup

Grilled Chicory Pears

CRUDITÉES WITH CHILLI TOMATO DIP

SERVES 4

One of the simplest yet most popular appetizers, an array of colourful, crisp vegetables served with a delicious dip is hard to resist.

2 celery sticks, trimmed and cut into
    eight pieces
1 green pepper, halved, seeded and
    cut into strips
1 carrot, cut into julienne sticks
3 cherry tomatoes
40 g (1½ oz) mangetout

For the dip
300 ml (½ pint) low-fat natural
    yogurt
15 ml (1 tbsp) tomato purée
60 ml (4 tbsp) low-fat mayonnaise
1 green chilli, chopped
15 g (1 tbsp) fresh chopped parsley

≈ Prepare all the vegetables. Mix together the dip ingredients and place in a serving bowl.

≈ Place the bowl on a serving platter and arrange the vegetables around the dip. Serve immediately.

BAKED POTATO SKINS

SERVES 4

Always a firm favourite, remember to prepare the skins a day in advance for ease and speed. Pop them into the oven to warm them through before serving.

≈ Scrub the potatoes and place on a baking sheet. Cook in the oven at 200°C (400°F, Gas 6) for 1 hour or until soft. Remove and cool. Cut the potatoes in half lengthways and scoop out the centres with a teaspoon, leaving a 1 cm (½ in) thickness shell. Sprinkle the skins with salt and place the potatoes in the oven for 10 minutes or until crisp.

≈ Mix the yogurt dip ingredients together. Mix together the mustard sauce ingredients. Finally mix the tomato salsa ingredients together. Place each dip in a separate bowl and cover until required. Serve with hot potato wedges.

NUTRITION FACTS	
Serving Size 1 (205g)	
Calories 105	Calories from Fat 18
	% Daily Value
Total Fat 2g	4%
Saturated Fat 1g	4%
Monounsaturated Fat 0.3g	0%
Polyunsaturated Fat 0.6g	0%
Cholesterol 4mg	1%
Sodium 330mg	14%
Total Carbohydrate 17g	6%
Dietary Fibre 3g	10%
Sugars 10g	0%
Protein 5g	0%

Per cent daily values are based on a 2000 calorie diet

Baked Potato Skins

4 medium baking potatoes

For the yogurt dip

150 ml (¼ pint) low-fat natural
    yogurt

2 garlic cloves, crushed

15 g (1 tbsp) spring onions, sliced

For the mustard sauce

150 ml (¼ pint) low-fat natural
    yogurt

10 ml (2 tsp) wholegrain mustard

1 jalapeño chilli, chopped

For the tomato salsa

2 medium tomatoes, chopped

45 g (3 tbsp) red onion, finely
    chopped

15 g (1 tbsp) fresh chopped parsley

1 green pepper, seeded and chopped

dash of sugar

NUTRITION FACTS	
Serving Size 1 (414g)	
Calories 325	Calories from Fat 18
	% Daily Value
Total Fat 2g	3%
Saturated Fat 1g	4%
Monounsaturated Fat 0.5g	0%
Polyunsaturated Fat 0.3g	0%
Cholesterol 4mg	1%
Sodium 107mg	4%
Total Carbohydrate 70g	23%
Dietary Fibre 7g	28%
Sugars 16g	0%
Protein 10g	0%

Per cent daily values are based on a 2000 calorie diet

2 flour tortillas

For the filling

115 g (4 oz) spinach, stems removed

4 spring onions, sliced

25 g (1 oz) low-fat vegetarian
    Cheddar cheese, grated

a pinch of ground coriander

1 small celery stick, trimmed and
    sliced

50 g (2 oz) drained, canned corn

1 carrot, peeled and grated

For the sauce

150 ml (¼ pint) skimmed milk

10 g (2 tbsp) cornflour

150 ml (¼ pint) vegetable stock

4 pickled jalapeño chillies, sliced

50 g (2 oz) low-fat vegetarian
    cheese, grated

15 ml (1 tbsp) tomato purée

15 g (1 tbsp) fresh chopped basil

basil or coriander sprigs to garnish

Vegetable Enchiladas

NUTRITION FACTS	
Serving Size 1 (221g)	
Calories 183	Calories from Fat 36
	% Daily Value
Total Fat 4g	6%
Saturated Fat 1g	6%
Monounsaturated Fat 1.0g	0%
Polyunsaturated Fat 0.7g	0%
Cholesterol 8mg	3%
Sodium 652mg	27%
Total Carbohydrate 25g	8%
Dietary Fibre 3g	12%
Sugars 5g	0%
Protein 13g	0%

Per cent daily values are based on a 2000 calorie diet

VEGETABLE KEBABS

SERVES 6

Perfect for vegetable lovers. This colourful combination of vegetables, marinated in vermouth, is served on a bed of bulgur wheat lightly flavoured with coriander.

≈ Prepare all the vegetables and place in a shallow dish. Mix together the vermouth, oil, 30 ml (2 tablespoons) of the lemon juice, garlic, half of the coriander and half of the lemon zest. Pour over the vegetables, cover and marinate for 2 hours.

≈ Meanwhile, place the bulgur wheat in a bowl, pour over 300 ml (½ pint) boiling water. Stand for 30 minutes or until the water is absorbed. Drain if necessary and stir in the remaining lemon juice and coriander. Season.

≈ Remove the vegetables from the marinade and thread on to four skewers. Grill for 10 minutes, turning until cooked through. Serve the bulgur wheat with the kebabs.

1 courgette, sliced

1 yellow pepper, seeded and cubed

4 baby corn, halved

4 button mushrooms

1 small red pepper, seeded and cubed

125 ml (4 fl oz) vermouth

15 ml (1 tbsp) olive oil

60 ml (4 tbsp) lemon juice

1 garlic clove, crushed

30 g (2 tbsp) fresh chopped coriander

grated zest of 1 lemon

115 g (4 oz) bulgur wheat

ground black pepper.

VEGETABLE ENCHILADAS

SERVES 4

This is a vegetarian version of the Mexican dish. Here, flour tortillas are filled with a mixture of crunchy vegetables, rolled and baked with a spicy tomato sauce. Pickled jalapeño chillies have been used as they are milder in flavour than fresh chillies.

≈ Blanch the spinach for the filling in boiling water for 2–3 minutes. Drain well and put in a mixing bowl with the onions, cheese, coriander, celery, corn and carrot.

≈ Spoon half of the filling along one edge of each of the tortillas. Roll up the tortillas and cut in half. Put in a shallow ovenproof baking dish, seam side down.

≈ For the sauce, blend 60 ml (4 tablespoons) of the skimmed milk to a paste with the cornflour. Heat the remaining milk and vegetable stock in a saucepan and stir in the cornflour paste, jalapeño chillies, half of the cheese and the tomato purée.

≈ Bring the sauce to the boil, stirring until thickened. Cook for 1 minute and pour over the tortillas in the dish. Sprinkle the remaining cheese on top and cook in the oven at 180°C (350°F, Gas 4) for 30 minutes or until the sauce is bubbling and the cheese has melted. Garnish with coriander or basil and serve with a small salad.

NUTRITION FACTS	
Serving Size 1 (209g)	
Calories 209	Calories from Fat 27
	% Daily Value
Total Fat 3g	5%
Saturated Fat 0g	2%
Monounsaturated Fat 1.7g	0%
Polyunsaturated Fat 0.3g	0%
Cholesterol 0mg	0%
Sodium 50mg	2%
Total Carbohydrate 33g	12%
Dietary Fibre 5g	19%
Sugars 2g	0%
Protein 4g	0%

Per cent daily values are based on a 2000 calorie diet

VEGETABLE AND BEAN SOUP

SERVES 8

This is a really hearty soup, filled with goodness. It may be made with any selection of vegetables you have to hand and is perfect for making ahead and freezing.

1.75 litres (3 pints) vegetable stock

1 onion, sliced

225 g (8 oz) potato, cubed

2 carrots, peeled and sliced

1 parsnip, peeled, cored, and chopped

1 leek, sliced

140 g (4½ oz) baby corn, sliced

2 garlic cloves, crushed

5 g (1 tsp) curry powder

5 g (1 tsp) chilli powder

450 g (16 oz) can red kidney beans, drained

450 g (16 oz) can borlotti or pinto beans, drained

ground black pepper

30 g (2 tbsp) fresh chopped parsley

≈ Heat 150 ml (¼ pint) of the stock in a large saucepan and cook the onion, potato, carrots, parsnip, leek, corn and garlic for 5 minutes.

≈ Add the curry and chilli powders with the remaining stock and bring the soup to the boil. Reduce the heat and simmer for 20 minutes or until the vegetables are tender. Add the drained beans and cook for a further 10 minutes. Season to taste and garnish with parsley before serving with crusty bread.

VEGETABLE JAMBALAYA

SERVES 4

This is a classic Caribbean dish, usually made with spicy sausage, but this vegetarian version packs just as much of a punch and tastes wonderful.

≈ Cook the rices in boiling water for 20 minutes or until cooked. Drain well.

≈ Meanwhile, place the aubergine pieces in a colander, sprinkle with the salt and leave to stand for 20 minutes. Wash and pat dry with absorbent kitchen paper.

≈ Put the aubergine, onion, celery and stock in a non-stick pan and cook for 5 minutes, stirring. Add the garlic, corn, beans, carrots, tomatoes, tomato purée, creole seasoning and chilli sauce. Bring the mixture to the boil, reduce the heat and cook for a further 20 minutes until the vegetables are just cooked. Stir in the drained rice and cook for a further 5 minutes. Garnish with parsley and serve.

NUTRITION FACTS	
Serving Size 1 (348g)	
Calories 275	Calories from Fat 18
	% Daily Value
Total Fat 2g	3%
Saturated Fat 0g	1%
Monounsaturated Fat 0.0g	0%
Polyunsaturated Fat 0.4g	0%
Cholesterol 0mg	0%
Sodium 980mg	41%
Total Carbohydrate 51g	17%
Dietary Fibre 11g	43%
Sugars 4g	0%
Protein 17g	0%

Per cent daily values are based on a 2000 calorie diet

Vegetable Jambalaya

45 g (1¾ oz) long grain white rice

40 g (1½ oz) wild rice

1 aubergine, sliced and quartered

5 g (1 tsp) salt

1 onion, chopped

1 celery stick, trimmed and sliced

175 ml (6 fl oz) vegetable stock

2 garlic cloves, crushed

40 g (1½ oz) baby corn

90 g (3½ oz) green beans, trimmed

175 g (6 oz) baby carrots

250 ml (8 fl oz) canned chopped
   tomatoes

20 ml (4 tsp) tomato purée

5 g (1 tsp) creole seasoning

5 g (1 tsp) chilli sauce

fresh chopped parsley to garnish

NUTRITION FACTS	
Serving Size 1 (228g)	
Calories 141	Calories from Fat 9
	% Daily Value
Total Fat 1g	**2%**
Saturated Fat 0g	1%
Monounsaturated Fat 0.1g	0%
Polyunsaturated Fat 0.5g	0%
Cholesterol 0mg	**0%**
Sodium 904mg	**38%**
Total Carbohydrate 29g	**10%**
Dietary Fibre 3g	11%
Sugars 3g	0%
Protein 6g	**0%**

Per cent daily values are based on a 2000 calorie diet

COURGETTE AND MINT SOUP

SERVES 4

This delicate soup may be served either hot or cold. If serving hot, stir in the yogurt once the soup has been liquidized, garnish and serve immediately with hot bread or croutons.

900 ml (1½ pints) vegetable stock

1 onion, chopped

1 garlic clove, crushed

3 courgettes, grated

1 large potato, scrubbed and chopped

15 g (1 tbsp) fresh chopped mint

ground black pepper

150 ml (¼ pint) low-fat natural yogurt

mint sprigs and courgette strips to garnish

NUTRITION FACTS

Serving Size 1 (271g)

Calories 78	Calories from Fat 9

	% Daily Value
Total Fat 1g	2%
Saturated Fat 0g	2%
Monounsaturated Fat 0.2g	0%
Polyunsaturated Fat 0.0g	0%
Cholesterol 2mg	1%
Sodium 821mg	34%
Total Carbohydrate 14g	5%
Dietary Fibre 1g	3%
Sugars 5g	0%
Protein 4g	0%

Per cent daily values are based on a 2000 calorie diet

≈ Put half of the vegetable stock in a large saucepan, add the onion and garlic and cook for 5 minutes over a gentle heat until the onion softens. Add the grated courgettes, potato and the remaining stock. Stir in the mint and cook over a gentle heat for 20 minutes or until the potato is cooked.

≈ Transfer the soup to a food processor and liquidize for 10 seconds, until almost smooth. Turn the soup into a bowl, season and stir in the yogurt. Cover and chill for 2 hours. Spoon the soup into individual serving bowls or a soup tureen, garnish and serve.

CHICORY AND ORANGE SALAD

SERVES 4

This recipe clears the palate for future courses. The crisp chicory is complemented by the fruit and tangy dressing.

2 oranges

2 heads chicory

1 pear

10 g (2 tsp) fresh chopped mint

15 ml (1 tbsp) clear honey

7.5 ml (½ tbsp) cider vinegar

30 ml (2 tbsp) orange juice

30 g (2 tbsp) walnuts, chopped

grated zest of 1 orange

NUTRITION FACTS

Serving Size 1 (179g)

Calories 109	Calories from Fat 27

	% Daily Value
Total Fat 3g	4%
Saturated Fat 0g	1%
Monounsaturated Fat 0.6g	0%
Polyunsaturated Fat 1.6g	0%
Cholesterol 0mg	0%
Sodium 12mg	0%
Total Carbohydrate 22g	7%
Dietary Fibre 4g	17%
Sugars 16g	0%
Protein 2g	0%

Per cent daily values are based on a 2000 calorie diet

≈ Peel the oranges and remove any pith. Separate the oranges into segments, reserving segments and any juice. Cut the chicory in half lengthways. Halve and slice the pear, removing the core.

≈ Mix together the mint, honey and vinegar. Add the orange juice and brush a little over the surface of the chicory. Cook under the grill for 2 minutes.

≈ Arrange the oranges and pear slices on a serving plate. Sprinkle with the chopped walnuts. Place the grilled chicory on serving plates and spoon on the remaining dressing. Sprinkle on orange zest and serve.

Courgette and Mint Soup ▶

SPINACH PÂTÉ

SERVES 8

This is a baked pâté which needs to be made well in advance of serving as it requires chilling after cooking. Be sure when draining the spinach to press out as much water as possible otherwise the mixture will be too wet. This recipe would be suitable for a lunch for four if sliced and served with salad or a tomato sauce.

40 g (1½ oz) bulgur wheat

675 g (1½ lb) spinach, stems removed

45 ml (3 tbsp) vegetable stock

1 onion, chopped

2 garlic cloves, crushed

15 g (1 tbsp) fresh chopped oregano

15 g (1 tbsp) fresh chopped thyme

10 ml (2 tsp) cider vinegar

1 egg, beaten

30 g (2 tbsp) fresh chopped coriander

50 g (2 oz) low-fat cheese, grated

6–8 large lettuce leaves

≈ Cook the bulgur wheat in boiling water for 15 minutes or until swollen and cooked. Drain well. Wash the spinach and cook in a saucepan until it begins to wilt. Drain very well and chop finely.

≈ Heat the stock in a saucepan and cook the onion and garlic for 2–3 minutes until beginning to soften. Add the bulgur wheat, oregano, thyme and vinegar and cook for 5 minutes. Remove the saucepan from the heat and stir in the egg, chopped coriander, cheese and spinach.

≈ Line a 900 g (2 lb) loaf tin with the lettuce leaves, allowing them to overhang the edge. Spoon the spinach mixture into the pan and fold the lettuce leaves over the top to cover the mixture completely.

≈ Cover the tin and cook the pâté in the oven at 180°C (350°F, Gas 4) for 45–60 minutes or until firm. Allow to cool before transferring to the refrigerator to chill for 2 hours. Unmould the pâté, slice and serve with hot toast and a small salad.

NUTRITION FACTS	
Serving Size 1 (138g)	
Calories 66	Calories from Fat 18
	% Daily Value
Total Fat 2g	2%
Saturated Fat 0g	2%
Monounsaturated Fat 0.4g	0%
Polyunsaturated Fat 0.2g	0%
Cholesterol 29mg	10%
Sodium 120mg	5%
Total Carbohydrate 8g	3%
Dietary Fibre 3g	13%
Sugars 1g	0%
Protein 6g	0%

Per cent daily values are based on a 2000 calorie diet

MEDITERRANEAN TOASTS

SERVES 4

These bite-sized hot open sandwiches are delicious as a snack or appetizer. Use a small crusty bread such as Italian ciabatta or a French stick if preferred, using eight slices in place of four. Be sure to cook these just before serving for full flavour.

4 large, thick slices of crusty bread

2 garlic cloves, crushed

15 ml (1 tbsp) low-fat polyunsaturated spread, melted

4 ripe tomatoes, peeled and chopped

15 ml (1 tbsp) tomato purée

4 stoned black olives, chopped

ground black pepper

basil sprigs to garnish

≈ Toast the slices of bread under the grill for 2 minutes each side. Mix the garlic and low-fat spread together and drizzle on to one side of the toasted bread.

≈ Mix the tomatoes, tomato purée and olives together, season, and spoon on to the toast. Cook under the grill for 2–3 minutes or until hot. Remove the toasts from under the grill and cut in half. Garnish with basil and serve.

NUTRITION FACTS	
Serving Size 1 (162g)	
Calories 123	Calories from Fat 27
	% Daily Value
Total Fat 3g	5%
‖‖‖‖‖‖‖‖‖‖‖ ‖‖‖ ‖‖‖	‖ ‖‖
Monounsaturated Fat 0.0g	0%
Polyunsaturated Fat 0.0g	0%
Cholesterol 0mg	0%
Sodium 265mg	11%
Total Carbohydrate 20g	7%
Dietary Fibre 2g	9%
Sugars 4g	0%
Protein 4g	0%

Per cent daily values are based on a 2000 calorie diet

Mediterranean Toasts ▶

MIXED BEAN
AND VEGETABLE SALAD

SERVES 4

Canned kidney beans and black-eyed beans are used in this colourful salad, but any beans you have to hand would be suitable. If you prefer to use dried beans, buy a mixed bag and soak 225 g (8 oz) overnight before cooking and draining thoroughly.

115 g (4 oz) lettuce

175 g (6 oz) canned red kidney beans, drained

175 g (6 oz) canned black-eyed beans, drained

1 red onion, halved and sliced

1 green pepper, seeded and cut into strips

1 orange pepper, seeded and cut into strips

155 g (4½ oz) baby corn

75 g (3 oz) broccoli florets

For the dressing

30 ml (2 tbsp) clear honey

30 ml (2 tbsp) garlic wine vinegar

10 ml (2 tsp) Dijon mustard

10 g (2 tsp) fresh chopped parsley

ground black pepper

≈ Line a salad bowl with the lettuce.
≈ Mix the beans, onion, peppers, corn and broccoli in a bowl and spoon into the lettuce lined bowl.

≈ Mix the dressing ingredients together in a screwtop jar, shake vigorously and pour over the salad. Toss well and serve with warm crusty bread.

CORN CHOWDER

SERVES 4

A classic chowder never loses its appeal. I challenge any of your guests to spot the difference in flavour from the traditional creamy recipe. Prepare in advance and freeze in convenient portion sizes for ease.

≈ Place the corn, stock, onion and pepper in a pan. Blend 60 ml (4 tablespoons) of the milk with the cornflour to form a paste.

≈ Bring the pan contents to the boil, reduce the heat and simmer for 20 minutes. Add the milk and cornflour paste and bring to the boil, stirring until thickened. Stir in the cheese and chives and season. Heat until the cheese has melted, garnish and serve.

NUTRITION FACTS	
Serving Size 1 (306g)	
Calories 482	Calories from Fat 18
	% Daily Value
Total Fat 2g	3%
Saturated Fat 0g	2%
Monounsaturated Fat 0.3g	0%
Polyunsaturated Fat 0.8g	0%
Cholesterol 0mg	0%
Sodium 309mg	13%
Total Carbohydrate 92g	31%
Dietary Fibre 20g	78%
Sugars 11g	0%
Protein 28g	0%

Per cent daily values are based on a 2000 calorie diet

275 g (10 oz) drained, canned corn
    kernels
600 ml (1 pint) vegetable stock
1 red onion, diced
1 green pepper, seeded and diced
600 ml (1 pint) skimmed milk
30 g (2 tbsp) cornflour
75 g (3 oz) low-fat Cheddar or Edam
    cheese, grated
15 g (1 tbsp) fresh snipped chives
ground black pepper
snipped chives, for garnish

NUTRITION FACTS	
Serving Size 1 (447g)	
Calories 216	Calories from Fat 36
	% Daily Value
Total Fat 4g	6%
Saturated Fat 1g	7%
Monounsaturated Fat 1.1g	0%
Polyunsaturated Fat 0.6g	0%
Cholesterol 10mg	3%
Sodium 854mg	36%
Total Carbohydrate 34g	11%
Dietary Fibre 2g	9%
Sugars 10g	0%
Protein 18g	0%

Per cent daily values are based on a 2000 calorie diet

Corn Chowder

41

200 g (7 oz) button mushrooms

125 ml (4 fl oz) dry sherry

60 ml (4 tbsp) garlic wine vinegar

60 ml (4 tbsp) vegetable stock

2 garlic cloves, crushed

1 onion, cut into eight

5 ml (1 tsp) mustard

15 ml (1 tbsp) soya sauce

30 ml (2 tbsp) tomato purée

1 bay leaf

NUTRITION FACTS

Serving Size 1 (103g)

Calories 44	Calories from Fat 9
	% Daily Value

Total Fat 1g	1%
Saturated Fat 0g	0%
Monounsaturated Fat 0.2g	0%
Polyunsaturated Fat 0.1g	0%
Cholesterol 0mg	0%
Sodium 368mg	15%
Total Carbohydrate 7g	2%
Dietary Fibre 1g	5%
Sugars 2g	0%
Protein 2g	0%

Per cent daily values are based on a 2000 calorie diet

For the sauce

3 red peppers, halved and seeded

475 ml (16 fl oz) vegetable stock

5 ml (1 tsp) chilli sauce

juice of 1 lemon

1 garlic clove, crushed

450 g (1 lb) asparagus spears, trimmed

grated zest of 1 lemon

parsley sprigs to garnish

NUTRITION FACTS

Serving Size 1 (303g)

Calories 57	Calories from Fat 9
	% Daily Value

Total Fat 1g	2%
Saturated Fat 0g	1%
Monounsaturated Fat 0.0g	0%
Polyunsaturated Fat 0.4g	0%
Cholesterol 0mg	0%
Sodium 937mg	39%
Total Carbohydrate 10g	3%
Dietary Fibre 3g	12%
Sugars 6g	0%
Protein 4g	0%

Per cent daily values are based on a 2000 calorie diet

MARINATED MUSHROOMS

SERVES 4

These mushrooms are quite spicy and are delicious served with oat cakes to mop up the delicious sauce.

≈ Place the mushrooms in a pan with the sherry, vinegar, stock, garlic, onion, mustard, soya sauce, tomato purée and bay leaf. Heat gently for 10 minutes. Allow to cool, remove bay leaf and transfer to a serving dish. Cover and chill until required. Serve with oat cakes and salad.

ASPARAGUS WITH RED PEPPER SAUCE

SERVES 4

This bright red pepper sauce looks terrific spooned over asparagus spears. If you don't want to make a spicy sauce, either reduce the amount of chilli sauce added, or omit it altogether.

≈ To make the sauce, cook the peppers under a hot grill, skin side uppermost for 5 minutes until the skin begins to blacken and blister. Transfer the peppers to a plastic bag using tongs, seal and leave for 20 minutes. Peel the skin from the peppers and discard.

≈ Roughly chop the peppers and put them in a saucepan with the stock, chilli sauce, lemon juice and garlic.

≈ Cook over a gentle heat for 20 minutes or until the peppers are tender. Transfer the sauce to a food processor and blend for 10 seconds. Return the purée to the saucepan and heat through gently.

≈ Meanwhile, tie the asparagus spears into four equal bundles. Stand upright in a steamer or saucepan filled with boiling water and cook for 10–15 minutes until tender. Remove the asparagus from the pan and untie the bundles. Arrange on four serving plates and spoon the sauce over the top. Sprinkle the lemon zest on top, garnish with parsley and serve.

Asparagus with Red Pepper Sauce ▶

MEDITERRANEAN SALAD

SERVES 4

A ny combination of vegetables would be delicious steeped in this tomato and garlic sauce. Be sure to chill the dish well before serving and have crusty bread to hand to mop up the juices.

300 ml (½ pint) vegetable stock

1 onion, finely chopped

1 garlic clove, crushed

60 ml (4 tbsp) dry white wine

4 tomatoes, peeled and chopped

juice of 1 lime

15 ml (1 tbsp) cider vinegar

10 ml (2 tsp) tomato purée

5 g (1 tsp) fennel seeds

5 g (1 tsp) mustard seeds

65 g (2½ oz) button mushrooms, quartered

50 g (2 oz) French beans, trimmed

1 courgette, sliced

ground black pepper

basil sprig to garnish

NUTRITION FACTS	
Serving Size 1 (311g)	
Calories 127	Calories from Fat 18
	% Daily Value
Total Fat 2g	3%
Saturated Fat 0g	1%
Monounsaturated Fat 0.3g	0%
Polyunsaturated Fat 0.4g	0%
Cholesterol 0mg	0%
Sodium 516mg	22%
Total Carbohydrate 23g	8%
Dietary Fibre 2g	8%
Sugars 6g	0%
Protein 6g	0%

Per cent daily values are based on a 2000 calorie diet

≈ Heat the stock in a large saucepan and cook the onion and garlic for 3–4 minutes. Add the wine, tomatoes, lime juice, vinegar, tomato purée, fennel and mustard seeds and the vegetables. Bring the mixture to the boil, reduce the heat and simmer for 20 minutes or until the vegetables are just cooked. Season with black pepper to taste.

≈ Transfer the mixture to a serving dish, cover and chill for at least 1 hour. Garnish with basil and serve.

PUMPKIN SOUP

SERVES 4

A filling soup, thickened with potato, this dish would also suffice as a light snack. Canned pumpkin is used for speed and ease.

≈ Place the onion, stock, potatoes and corn in a large pan. Cook for 15 minutes until the potatoes are tender.

≈ Add the canned pumpkin, milk and half of the chives. Cook for 5 minutes. Ladle into serving bowls, sprinkle with the remaining chives and serve.

1 small onion, chopped

475 ml (16 fl oz) vegetable stock

175 g (6 oz) potatoes, diced

225 g (8 oz) drained, canned corn kernels

450 g (1 lb) can of pumpkin

300 ml (½ pint) skimmed milk

30 g (2 tbsp) fresh snipped chives

NUTRITION FACTS	
Serving Size 1 (426g)	
Calories 187	Calories from Fat 18
	% Daily Value
Total Fat 2g	3%
Saturated Fat 1g	3%
Monounsaturated Fat 0.6g	0%
Polyunsaturated Fat 0.5g	0%
Cholesterol 1mg	0%
Sodium 657mg	27%
Total Carbohydrate 37g	12%
Dietary Fibre 6g	23%
Sugars 6g	0%
Protein 9g	0%

Per cent daily values are based on a 2000 calorie diet

GRILLED CHICORY PEARS

SERVES 6

Chicory has a slightly bitter flavour which is complemented perfectly by the sweetness of the pears in this recipe. Prepare and cook this dish just before serving as the chicory browns quickly if cut and allowed to stand.

≈ Cut the chicory heads in half lengthways. Mix half of the oil with the garlic and brush all over the chicory. Cook under a hot grill for 3–4 minutes or until the chicory begins to colour. Turn the chicory halves over and cook for a further 1–2 minutes.

≈ Carefully turn the chicory again and top each piece with the sliced pear. Mix the remaining oil with the lemon juice and thyme, season and brush over the pears and chicory. Cook under the hot grill for 3–4 minutes until the pears begin to colour, and transfer to warmed serving plates. Scatter the chestnuts over the top and spoon the lemon juice onto the pears. Sprinkle with lemon zest and garnish with fresh thyme sprigs. Serve immediately with hot crusty bread.

4 small heads of chicory

20 ml (4 tsp) sunflower oil

1 garlic clove, crushed

2 ripe dessert pears, halved, cored, and sliced

15 ml (1 tbsp) lemon juice

10 g (2 tsp) fresh chopped thyme

ground black pepper

50 g (2 oz) peeled chestnuts, cooked and chopped

lemon juice, lemon zest, and thyme sprigs to serve

NUTRITION FACTS	
Serving Size 1 (106g)	
Calories 112	Calories from Fat 27
	% Daily Value
Total Fat 3g	5%
Saturated Fat 0g	2%
Monounsaturated Fat 1.5g	0%
Polyunsaturated Fat 1.3g	0%
Cholesterol 0mg	0%
Sodium 20mg	1%
Total Carbohydrate 20g	7%
Dietary Fibre 1g	6%
Sugars 8g	0%
Protein 1g	0%

Per cent daily values are based on a 2000 calorie diet

LIGHT LUNCHES AND SUPPERS

Curried Lentil Pâté

Roasted Vegetables on Toast

Spinach Crêpes

Pasta Caponata

Chestnut Hash

Aubergine-stuffed Mushrooms

Spinach and Carrot Mousse

Vegetable Calzone

Stuffed Lettuce Leaves

Bean and Asparagus Fry

Garlic Aubergine Rolls

Chinese Noodles

CURRIED LENTIL PÂTÉ

SERVES 8

750 ml (1¼ pints) vegetable stock

1 onion, chopped

3 garlic cloves, crushed

5 g (1 tsp) ground cumin

5 g (1 tsp) ground coriander

2.5 g (½ tsp) chilli powder

200 g (7 oz) red split lentils, washed

1 egg

60 ml (4 tbsp) skimmed milk

30 ml (2 tbsp) peach relish

30 g (2 tbsp) fresh chopped
    coriander

ground black pepper

coriander sprigs to garnish

*R*ed *lentils are used for speed in this recipe as they do not require pre-soaking. Should you wish to use other lentils, wash and soak them well and cook before using in the recipe.*

≈ Heat 150 ml (¼ pint) of the vegetable stock in a saucepan and cook the onion and garlic for 2–3 minutes or until the onion begins to soften. Add the ground cumin, ground coriander, chilli powder, lentils and the remaining stock. Bring the mixture to the boil, then reduce the heat and simmer for 20 minutes or until the lentils are soft and cooked. Remove the pan from the heat and drain well.

≈ Transfer the mixture to a food processor and add the egg, milk, relish, chopped coriander and black pepper to taste. Blend for 10 seconds until smooth. Spoon into a non-stick 900 g (2 lb) loaf tin and smooth the surface with the back of a spoon. Cover and cook in the oven at 200°C (400°F, Gas 6) for 1 hour or until firm to the touch.

≈ Allow the pâté to cool before transferring to the refrigerator to chill. Unmould the pâté, slice, garnish with coriander and serve with a crisp salad.

ROASTED VEGETABLES ON TOAST

SERVES 4

*T*he *flavour of roasted vegetables is quite different from that achieved by boiling or steaming, and one not to be missed. This Mediterranean mixture is really colourful and tastes great with the light cheese sauce.*

≈ Heat the oven to 200°C (400°F, Gas 6). Blanch all of the vegetables in boiling water for 8 minutes and drain well. Transfer the vegetables to a roasting tin and sprinkle the oil and rosemary over the top. Cook in the oven for 25 minutes or until softened and beginning to char slightly.

≈ Meanwhile, heat the broth for the sauce in a pan with the milk. Add the garlic, cream cheese, ground black pepper and mustard. Blend the cornflour

with 30 ml (2 tablespoons) of cold water to form a paste and stir into the sauce. Bring to the boil, stirring until thickened and add the rosemary.

≈ Cook the bread under the grill for 2–3 minutes each side until golden. Arrange two slices of the toast on four warmed serving plates and top with the roast vegetables. Spoon on the sauce, garnish with basil and rosemary and serve.

NUTRITION FACTS	
Serving Size 1 (139g)	
Calories 107	Calories from Fat 9
	% Daily Value
Total Fat 1g	2%
Saturated Fat 0g	1%
Monounsaturated Fat 0.3g	0%
Polyunsaturated Fat 0.2g	0%
Cholesterol 27mg	9%
Sodium 414mg	17%
Total Carbohydrate 17g	6%
Dietary Fibre 7g	28%
Sugars 4g	0%
Protein 8g	0%

Per cent daily values are based on a 2000 calorie diet

1 head of fennel, trimmed and
  quartered
2 open cap flat mushrooms, peeled
  and sliced
1 courgette, sliced
1 red pepper, seeded, halved, and
  sliced
1 red onion, cut into eight pieces
15 ml (1 tbsp) sunflower oil
2 rosemary sprigs
8 small slices of thick wholemeal
  bread

For the sauce
150 ml (¼ pint) vegetable stock
75 ml (3 fl oz) skimmed milk
2 garlic cloves, crushed
50 g (2 oz) low-fat cream cheese
ground black pepper
5 ml (1 tsp) Dijon mustard
15 g (1 tbsp) cornflour
1 rosemary sprig, chopped
basil and rosemary sprigs to garnish

Roasted Vegetables on Toast

NUTRITION FACTS	
Serving Size 1 (245g)	
Calories 250	Calories from Fat 72
	% Daily Value
Total Fat 8g	12%
Saturated Fat 1g	4%
Monounsaturated Fat 1.9g	0%
Polyunsaturated Fat 1.5g	0%
Cholesterol 9mg	3%
Sodium 420mg	18%
Total Carbohydrate 43g	14%
Dietary Fibre 7g	28%
Sugars 3g	0%
Protein 13g	0%

Per cent daily values are based on a 2000 calorie diet

SPINACH CRÊPES

SERVES 4

These unusual light crêpes are made from a low-fat dough and rolled out. Keep an eye on them during cooking as they can quickly brown.

For the crêpes

75 g (3 oz) plain flour
125 ml (4 fl oz) water
5 ml (1 tsp) sunflower oil

For the filling

30 ml (2 tbsp) vegetable stock
1 small courgette, sliced
50 g (2 oz) spinach, shredded
1 small onion, chopped
65 g (2½ oz) button mushrooms, sliced
½ red pepper, seeded and cut into strips
1 celery stick, sliced
1 garlic clove, crushed
a pinch of ground nutmeg

For the sauce

150 ml (¼ pint) skimmed milk
15 g (1 tbsp) cornflour
150 ml (¼ pint) vegetable stock
ground black pepper
15 g (1 tbsp) fresh chopped thyme
50 g (2 oz) low-fat vegetarian cheese, grated
2.5 g (½ tsp) paprika

≈ Sieve the flour for the crêpes into a mixing bowl and make a well in the centre. Heat the water and oil to boiling point and pour into the flour, mixing to form a dough. Turn on to a floured surface and knead for 3–4 minutes.

≈ Cut the mixture into four equal portions and roll each into a 15 cm (6 in) round. Heat a heavy, non-stick frying pan over medium heat. Put one of the crêpes into the pan and place another on top. Cook for 3–4 minutes, turning once when the bottom crêpe begins to brown. Cover the cooked crêpes with a clean, damp teatowel and repeat with remaining mixture. Cover and reserve.

≈ Heat the stock for the filling in a saucepan and cook the vegetables, garlic, and nutmeg for 7–8 minutes, stirring. Drain the mixture well.

≈ Blend 30 ml (2 tablespoons) of the milk for the sauce to a paste with the cornflour. Put in a saucepan with the remaining milk, vegetable stock, seasoning, thyme and half of the cheese. Bring the mixture to the boil, stirring until thickened.

≈ Heat the oven to 190°C (375°F, Gas 5). Spoon the vegetable mixture on to one half of each crêpe and roll up. Put in a shallow ovenproof dish, seam side down. Pour the sauce over the top and sprinkle with the remaining cheese and paprika. Cook in the oven for 15 minutes until golden brown. Serve immediately with salad.

NUTRITION FACTS	
Serving Size 1 (267g)	
Calories 174	Calories from Fat 27
	% Daily Value
Total Fat 3g	4%
Saturated Fat 0g	2%
Monounsaturated Fat 0.6g	0%
Polyunsaturated Fat 0.7g	0%
Cholesterol 1mg	0%
Sodium 390mg	16%
Total Carbohydrate 32g	11%
Dietary Fibre 2g	6%
Sugars 4g	0%
Protein 7g	0%

Per cent daily values are based on a 2000 calorie diet

PASTA CAPONATA

SERVES 4

Caponata is a well-known tomato and vegetable dish which is perfect to serve hot as a low-fat pasta sauce. In this recipe dried penne has been used but any pasta shapes or noodles would work equally well.

1 large aubergine

salt

150 ml (¼ pint) vegetable stock

1 onion, halved and sliced

2 garlic cloves, crushed

475 ml (16 fl oz) plum tomatoes, chopped

30 ml (2 tbsp) cider vinegar

4 celery sticks, chopped

50 g (2 oz) green beans, trimmed

25 g (1 oz) stoned green olives, halved

15 g (1 tbsp) fresh chopped basil

ground black pepper

225 g (8 oz) dried penne

basil sprigs to garnish

≈ Cut the aubergine into chunks and put in a colander. Sprinkle with salt and leave to stand for 20 minutes. Wash under cold water and pat dry. Cook the aubergine under a medium grill for 5 minutes, turning until browned.

≈ Meanwhile, heat the stock in a saucepan and add the onion and garlic. Cook for 2–3 minutes until softened. Stir in the tomatoes, vinegar, celery and beans. Cook over a gentle heat for 20 minutes, stirring occasionally. Add the aubergine, olives, and basil, season and cook for a further 10 minutes.

≈ Meanwhile, cook the penne in boiling salted water for 8–10 minutes or until just tender. Drain well and toss into the sauce. Spoon into a warmed serving dish, garnish with basil and serve.

NUTRITION FACTS	
Serving Size 1 (342g)	
Calories 324	Calories from Fat 27
	% Daily Value
Total Fat 3g	5%
Saturated Fat 0g	1%
Monounsaturated Fat 1.0g	0%
Polyunsaturated Fat 0.8g	0%
Cholesterol 0mg	0%
Sodium 222mg	14%
Total Carbohydrate 61g	11%
Dietary Fibre 5g	20%
Sugars 6g	0%
Protein 12g	0%

Per cent daily values are based on a 2000 calorie diet

CHESTNUT HASH

SERVES 4

Cook the potatoes for this dish in advance or use up any leftover cooked potatoes for speed. Allow the potato to brown on the base of the pan for a crunchier texture.

675 g (1½ lb) potatoes, peeled and cubed

1 red onion, halved and sliced

75 g (3 oz) mangetout

50 g (2 oz) broccoli florets

1 courgette, sliced

1 green pepper, seeded and sliced

40 g (1½ oz) drained, canned corn

2 garlic cloves, crushed

5 g (1 tsp) paprika

30 g (2 tbsp) fresh chopped parsley

150 ml (¼ pint) vegetable stock

25 g (1 oz) chestnuts, cooked, peeled and quartered

ground black pepper

parsley sprigs to garnish

≈ Cook the potatoes in boiling water for 20 minutes or until softened. Drain well and reserve.

≈ Meanwhile, cook the remaining ingredients in a frying pan for 10 minutes, stirring. Add the drained potatoes to the pan and cook for a further 15 minutes, stirring and pressing down with the back of a spoon. Serve immediately with crusty bread.

NUTRITION FACTS	
Serving Size 1 (396g)	
Calories 247	Calories from Fat 9
	% Daily Value
Total Fat 1g	2%
Saturated Fat 0g	1%
Monounsaturated Fat 0.2g	0%
Polyunsaturated Fat 0.3g	0%
Cholesterol 0mg	0%
Sodium 431mg	18%
Total Carbohydrate 55g	18%
Dietary Fibre 5g	22%
Sugars 8g	0%
Protein 7g	0%

Per cent daily values are based on a 2000 calorie diet

AUBERGINE-STUFFED MUSHROOMS

SERVES 4

Make the aubergine purée in advance for this recipe and store in the refrigerator for up to one day.

1 aubergine

2 garlic cloves, crushed

juice of 1 lime

1 cup wholemeal breadcrumbs

15 ml (1 tbsp) tomato purée

15 g (1 tbsp) fresh chopped
   coriander

8 large open cap mushrooms, peeled

25 g (1 oz) low-fat vegetarian
   cheese, grated

60 ml (4 tbsp) vegetable stock

coriander sprigs to garnish

≈ Heat the oven to 220°C (425°F, Gas 7). Cut the aubergine in half lengthways and place skin side uppermost in a baking dish. Cook in the oven for 30 minutes until soft. Remove the aubergine from the oven and allow to cool. Scoop the soft flesh from the skin and put in a food processor with the garlic and lime juice. Add the breadcrumbs to the food processor with the tomato purée and coriander and blend for 10 seconds to mix well.

≈ Spoon the purée on to the mushrooms pressing the mixture down. Sprinkle the cheese on top and transfer the mushrooms to a shallow ovenproof dish. Pour the stock around the mushrooms, cover and cook in the oven for 20 minutes. Remove the cover and cook for a further 5 minutes until golden on top.

Remove the mushrooms from the oven and from the dish with a draining spoon. Serve with a mixed salad and garnish with coriander.

NUTRITION FACTS	
Serving Size 1 (128g)	
Calories 161	Calories from Fat 27
	% Daily Value
Total Fat 3g	5%
Saturated Fat 1g	3%
Monounsaturated Fat 1.4g	0%
Polyunsaturated Fat 0.7g	0%
Cholesterol 0mg	0%
Sodium 389mg	16%
Total Carbohydrate 1.1g	0%
Dietary Fibre 3g	12%
Sugars 1g	0%
Protein 6g	0%

Per cent daily values are based on a 2000 calorie diet

SPINACH AND CARROT MOUSSE

SERVES 8

This is an impressive dish which is deceiving as it is so simple. It is ideal for entertaining as it may be made in advance and chilled.

450 g (1 lb) spinach, stalks removed

5 g (1 tsp) ground ginger

5 g (1 tsp) curry powder

1 onion, chopped

425 g (15 oz) carrots, grated

2 garlic cloves, crushed

60 ml (4 tbsp) vegetable stock

4 egg whites

courgette strips to garnish

≈ Wash the spinach and cook, covered, in a large saucepan on a low heat for 5 minutes until wilted. Drain very well, squeezing out as much liquid as possible and blend in a food processor with the ginger and curry powder for 10 seconds. Transfer the purée to a mixing bowl.

≈ Cook the onion, carrots and garlic in the stock for 10 minutes or until the carrots are soft. Put in a food processor and liquidize for 10 seconds. Transfer to a separate mixing bowl.

≈ Whisk the egg whites until peaking and fold half into each of the vegetable purées. Spoon half of the carrot mixture into the base of a non-stick 900 g (2 lb) loaf tin, top with half of the spinach mixture and repeat once more. Cover and stand in a roasting tin half filled with boiling water.

≈ Heat the oven to 180°C (350°F, Gas 4). Cook the mousse for 1 hour or until set. Leave to cool and then transfer to the fridge to chill completely. Turn the mousse on to a serving plate, arrange courgette strips around the base and serve.

VEGETABLE CALZONE

SERVES 4

Calzone or pizza dough pasties are perfect for filling with your favourite ingredients. In this recipe the dough is slightly sweetened with honey for added flavour, but seeds or herbs could be added to the dough, or even garlic for variety.

≈ Sift the flour for the dough into a large mixing bowl. Add the yeast and make a well in the centre. Stir in the honey and stock and bring together to a dough. Turn the dough on to a lightly floured surface and knead for 10 minutes until smooth and elastic. Put in a mixing bowl, cover, and leave in a warm place to prove for 1 hour or until doubled in size.

≈ Meanwhile, heat the stock for the filling in a saucepan and stir in the tomatoes, basil, garlic, tomato purée, celery and leek and cook for 5 minutes, stirring.

≈ Divide the risen dough into four equal pieces. Roll each out on a lightly floured surface to a circle 18 cm (7 in) in diameter. Spoon equal amounts of the filling on to one half of each dough circle. Sprinkle with cheese. Brush the edge with milk and fold the dough over to form four semicircles. Crimp the seams, pressing together to seal and transfer the calzone to a non-stick baking sheet. Brush with milk.

≈ Heat the oven to 220°C (425°F, Gas 7). Cook the calzone for 30 minutes until risen and golden. Serve with salad.

NUTRITION FACTS	
Serving Size 1 (166g)	
Calories 49	Calories from Fat 9
	% Daily Value
Total Fat 1g	1%
Saturated Fat 0g	0%
Monounsaturated Fat 0.0g	0%
Polyunsaturated Fat 0.1g	0%
Cholesterol 0mg	0%
Sodium 208mg	9%
Total Carbohydrate 6g	2%
Dietary Fibre 3g	13%
Sugars 1g	0%
Protein 7g	0%

Per cent daily values are based on a 2000 calorie diet

Vegetable Calzone

For the dough

450 g (1 lb) white bread flour

5 g (1 tsp) easy-blend dried yeast

15 ml (1 tbsp) clear honey

300 ml (½ pint) vegetable stock

skimmed milk for glazing

For the filling

125 ml (4 fl oz) vegetable stock

40 g (1½ oz) sundried tomatoes,
   chopped

30 g (2 tbsp) fresh chopped basil

2 garlic cloves, crushed

30 ml (2 tbsp) tomato purée

1 celery stick, sliced

1 leek, sliced

25 g (1 oz) low-fat vegetarian
   cheese, grated

NUTRITION FACTS	
Serving Size 1 (332g)	
Calories 584	Calories from Fat 45
	% Daily Value
Total Fat 5g	8%
Saturated Fat 0g	2%
Monounsaturated Fat 0.4g	0%
Polyunsaturated Fat 0.5g	0%
Cholesterol 0mg	0%
Sodium 653mg	27%
Total Carbohydrate 110g	36%
Dietary Fibre 3g	13%
Sugars 9g	0%
Protein 25g	0%

Per cent daily values are based on a 2000 calorie diet

STUFFED LETTUCE LEAVES

SERVES 4

These small lettuce parcels are packed with a spicy vegetable and rice filling, then baked with a tomato sauce for a complete meal in itself. Make the filling and the sauce in advance and assemble the dish just before required. The recipe would also adequately serve eight as an appetizer, with only one parcel per person.

300 ml (½ pint) vegetable stock

1 red onion, chopped

2 garlic cloves, crushed

65 g (2½ oz) button mushrooms, chopped

50 g (2 oz) brown rice

50 g (2 oz) drained, canned corn

5 g (1 tsp) curry powder

8 large, firm lettuce leaves such as iceberg or Cos

For the sauce

475 ml (16 fl oz) passata

5 ml (1 tsp) light soya sauce

2.5 ml (½ tsp) chilli sauce

15 g (1 tbsp) fresh chopped basil

5 g (1 tsp) light brown sugar

ground black pepper

≈ Heat 75 ml (5 tablespoons) of the vegetable stock in a saucepan, add the onion and garlic and cook for 3–4 minutes until the onion begins to soften. Stir in the mushrooms, rice, corn, curry powder and remaining stock, bring to the boil, reduce the heat and simmer for 30–40 minutes until the rice is cooked and the liquid has been absorbed.

≈ Meanwhile, mix all of the sauce ingredients in a pan and bring to the boil. Reduce the heat, cover, and simmer for 10 minutes.

≈ Heat the oven to 180°C (350°F, Gas 4). Place the lettuce leaves on a chopping board and spoon equal quantities of the rice filling into the centre of each. Wrap the leaves around the filling and place seam side down in an ovenproof dish. Spoon the sauce over the top and cook in the oven for 10 minutes. Serve immediately.

NUTRITION FACTS	
Serving Size 1 (288g)	
Calories 87	Calories from Fat 9
	% Daily Value
Total Fat 1g	1%
Saturated Fat 0g	0%
Monounsaturated Fat 0.1g	0%
Polyunsaturated Fat 0.2g	0%
Cholesterol 0mg	0%
Sodium 771mg	32%
Total Carbohydrate 19g	6%
Dietary Fibre 2g	6%
Sugars 6g	0%
Protein 3g	0%

Per cent daily values are based on a 2000 calorie diet

BEAN AND ASPARAGUS FRY

SERVES 4

Fresh green beans and tender young asparagus are complemented in this recipe by a honey and lime-based sauce. Use any mixture of green beans that you have to hand for a quick and delicious dish.

≈ Top and tail the beans and cut into 2.5 cm (1 in) slices, if necessary. Mix the beans and asparagus together.

≈ Heat the stock in a large frying pan and add the vegetables, honey, lime juice, pepper, garlic, fennel seeds and mustard. Cook, stirring for 7–8 minutes until the vegetables are cooked but crisp. Stir in the cheese and parsley and serve immediately.

225 g (8 oz) mixed fresh beans (e.g. green, wax, or French beans)

225 g (8 oz) young asparagus spears

75 g (3 oz) shelled broad beans

125 ml (4 fl oz) vegetable stock

30 ml (2 tbsp) clear honey

15 ml (1 tbsp) lime juice

ground black pepper

3 garlic cloves, crushed

5 g (1 tsp) fennel seeds

5 ml (1 tsp) Dijon mustard

25 g (1 oz) low-fat vegetarian cheese, grated

30 g (2 tbsp) fresh chopped parsley

Bean and Asparagus Fry

NUTRITION FACTS	
Serving Size 1 (196g)	
Calories 295	Calories from Fat 27
	% Daily Value
Total Fat 3g	5%
Saturated Fat 0g	2%
Monounsaturated Fat 1.0g	0%
Polyunsaturated Fat 1.0g	0%
Cholesterol 0mg	0%
Sodium 509mg	21%
Total Carbohydrate 53g	11%
Dietary Fibre 10g	39%
Sugars 12g	0%
Protein 18g	0%

Per cent daily values are based on a 2000 calorie diet

GARLIC AUBERGINE ROLLS

SERVES 8

These may take a little preparation but they are well worth the effort. Cooking garlic in its skin takes away the strong flavour and produces a milder garlic purée. This can be cooked in advance with the aubergine and gently warmed through to make the rolls.

8 garlic cloves

1 aubergine, sliced

15 ml (1 tbsp) sunflower oil

25 g (1 oz) sundried tomatoes, reconstituted and sliced

30 g (2 tbsp) basil leaves, shredded

4 lettuce leaves, shredded

4 ciabatta or crusty large rolls

≈ Heat the oven to 200°C (400°F, Gas 6). Put the garlic and aubergine slices on a non-stick baking sheet and cook in the oven for 30 minutes until soft. Remove from the oven and cool.

≈ Squeeze the garlic purée from the cloves and reserve. Mix the tomatoes, basil and lettuce leaves together. Heat the rolls in a warm oven for 2–3 minutes and slice in half. Spread the garlic purée on to one half of each roll and top with the aubergine slices. Add the tomato mixture and top with remaining roll halves. Serve hot.

NUTRITION FACTS

Serving Size 1 (83g)

Calories 132	Calories from Fat 27
	% Daily Value
Total Fat 3g	5%
Saturated Fat 0g	2%
Monounsaturated Fat 1.3g	0%
Polyunsaturated Fat 0.2g	0%
Cholesterol 0mg	0%
Sodium 166mg	7%
Total Carbohydrate 23g	8%
Dietary Fibre 1g	5%
Sugars 0g	0%
Protein 4g	0%

Per cent daily values are based on a 2000 calorie diet

CHINESE NOODLES

SERVES 4

This is a really quick and easy dish for a speedy lunch or supper. Use egg or rice noodles for a Chinese flavour or pasta ribbons if preferred, but these will require cooking for 8–10 minutes.

225 g (8 oz) thin egg or rice noodles
75 ml (3 fl oz) vegetable stock
2 garlic cloves, crushed
1 red onion, halved and sliced
2.5 cm (1 in) piece of root ginger, grated
1 red chilli, chopped
2 carrots, cut into strips
50 g (2 oz) sugar snap peas
1 courgette, sliced
1 celery stick, sliced
5 g (1 tsp) curry powder
45 ml (3 tbsp) dark soya sauce
45 ml (3 tbsp) plum sauce
5 g (1 tsp) fennel seeds
fresh chopped parsley or fennel leaves to garnish

≈ Cook the noodles in boiling water for 3 minutes. Drain and reserve. Meanwhile, heat the stock in a non-stick wok or frying pan and cook the vegetables and spices for 3–4 minutes, stirring constantly.

≈ Add the drained noodles to the pan with the soya and plum sauces and the fennel seeds. Cook for 2–3 minutes, tossing well and serve garnished with parsley or fennel leaves.

NUTRITION FACTS	
Serving Size 1 (265g)	
Calories 139	Calories from Fat 9
	% Daily Value
Total Fat 1g	1%
Saturated Fat 0g	1%
Monounsaturated Fat 0.2g	0%
Polyunsaturated Fat 0.1g	0%
Cholesterol 0mg	0%
Sodium 1004mg	42%
Total Carbohydrate 31g	11%
Dietary Fibre 4g	14%
Sugars 9g	0%
Protein 4g	0%

Per cent daily values are based on a 2000 calorie diet

VEGETABLE LASAGNE

SERVES 4

This is a low fat version of a classic dish using a colourful mixture of vegetables to replace the meat. Serve with salad for a delicious combination.

1 small aubergine
salt
450 g (16 oz) can chopped tomatoes
2 garlic cloves, crushed
15 g (1 tbsp) chopped basil
1 large courgette, seeded and
    chopped
1 onion, chopped
1 green pepper, seeded and chopped
65 g (2½ oz) button mushrooms,
    sliced
5 g (1 tsp) chilli powder
ground black pepper
115 g (4 oz) lasagne verdi (no
    pre-cook variety)

For the sauce
150 ml (¼ pint) vegetable stock
300 ml (½ pint) skimmed milk
50 g (2 oz) low fat vegetarian
    cheese, grated
5 ml (1 tsp) Dijon mustard
30 g (2 tbsp) cornflour
15 g (1 tbsp) fresh chopped basil

≈ Slice the aubergine and put in a colander. Sprinkle with salt and leave for 30 minutes. Wash and pat dry.
≈ Put the tomatoes, garlic, basil, courgette, onion, pepper, mushrooms and chilli powder in a saucepan. Add the aubergine and cook for 30 minutes, stirring occasionally until the vegetables are cooked.
≈ Mix the stock for the sauce, the milk, half of the cheese and the mustard in a saucepan. Blend the cornflour with

60 ml (4 tablespoons) cold water to form a paste and add to the pan. Bring to the boil, stirring until thickened.
≈ Spoon a layer of the vegetable mixture into the base of an ovenproof dish. Lay half of the lasagne on top to cover. Spoon on remaining vegetable mixture and cover with the remaining lasagne. Pour the cheese sauce over the top and cook at 190°C (375°F, Gas 5) for 40 minutes or until golden and bubbling. Sprinkle the basil on top and serve.

VEGETABLE AND TOFU PIE

SERVES 8

In this recipe, firm tofu (bean curd) is cubed and added to the pie. If liked, use a marinated tofu for extra flavour and use in the same way.

≈ Place all of the vegetables and the tofu in a non-stick frying pan and dry fry for 3–5 minutes, stirring. Add the stock and coriander, season and cook for 20 minutes or until the vegetables are tender. Blend the cornflour to a paste with 30 ml (2 tablespoons) of cold water, add to the mixture and bring the mixture to the boil, stirring until thickened.

≈ Spoon the mixture into an ovenproof pie dish. Lay one sheet of filo pastry on top and brush with melted fat. Cut the remaining pastry into strips and lay on top, folding as you go to create a rippled effect. Sprinkle the remaining fat on top and cook the pie in the oven at 200°C (400°F, Gas 6) for 20 minutes until golden brown. Serve with new potatoes.

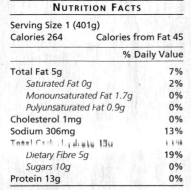

NUTRITION FACTS	
Serving Size 1 (401g)	
Calories 264	Calories from Fat 45
	% Daily Value
Total Fat 5g	7%
Saturated Fat 0g	2%
Monounsaturated Fat 1.7g	0%
Polyunsaturated Fat 0.9g	0%
Cholesterol 1mg	0%
Sodium 306mg	13%
Total Carbohydrate 19g	11%
Dietary Fibre 5g	19%
Sugars 10g	0%
Protein 13g	0%

Per cent daily values are based on a 2000 calorie diet

Classic Vegetable Dishes and Casseroles

Vegetable Lasagne

Vegetable and Tofu Pie

Mixed Bean Chilli

Vegetable Flan

Stuffed Pasta Shells

Wild Rice and Lentil Casserole

Spicy Chick-peas

Winter Vegetable Casserole

Roast Pepper Tart

Pasta Timbale

Saffron Rice and Vegetables

Vegetable Pilaff

Vegetable Risotto

Vegetable Chop Suey

Tofu Burgers and Chips

MIXED BEAN CHILLI

SERVES 4

Chilli con carne has always been a warming favourite, and this recipe without the "carne" is no exception. Packed with vegetables and beans, it is a fully satisfying meal.

450 g (16 oz) canned beans such as
    borlotti, red kidney, black-eyed
    and pinto beans, drained

400 g (14 oz) can chopped tomatoes

15 ml (1 tbsp) tomato purée

1 onion, halved and sliced

150 g (5 oz) potatoes, cubed

1 green pepper, seeded and chopped

150 g (5 oz) baby corn, halved

2 green chillies, seeded and chopped

5 g (1 tsp) chilli powder

2 garlic cloves, crushed

150 ml (¼ pint) vegetable stock

fresh chopped parsley to garnish

NUTRITION FACTS	
Serving Size 1 (351g)	
Calories 178	Calories from Fat 9
	% Daily Value
Total Fat 1g	2%
Saturated Fat 0g	1%
Monounsaturated Fat 0.2g	0%
Polyunsaturated Fat 0.3g	0%
Cholesterol 0mg	0%
Total Carbohydrate 36g	12%
Dietary Fibre 7g	30%
Sugars 5g	0%
Protein 8g	0%

Per cent daily values are based on a 2000 calorie diet

≈ Place all of the ingredients except the garnish in a large saucepan and bring to the boil. Reduce the heat, cover the pan and simmer for 15 minutes or until all of the vegetables are cooked and the juices have thickened slightly. Stir the chilli occasionally while cooking.

≈ Garnish with parsley and serve with brown rice or baked potatoes.

4 sheets of filo pastry

15 ml (1 tbsp) polyunsaturated
low-fat spread, melted

For the filling

1 leek, sliced

2 garlic cloves, crushed

2 carrots, diced

115 g (4 oz) cauliflower florets

115 g (4 oz) French beans, halved

2 celery sticks, sliced

225 g (8 oz) firm tofu, diced

300 ml (½ pint) vegetable stock

30 g (2 tbsp) fresh chopped
coriander

ground black pepper

15 g (1 tbsp) cornflour

Vegetable and Tofu Pie

NUTRITION FACTS	
Serving Size 1 (152g)	
Calories 130	Calories from Fat 27
	% Daily Value
Total Fat 3g	4%
Saturated Fat 0g	2%
Monounsaturated Fat 0.6g	0%
Polyunsaturated Fat 1.3g	0%
Cholesterol 0mg	0%
Sodium 257mg	11%
Total Carbohydrate 21g	7%
Dietary Fibre 1g	5%
Sugars 3g	0%
Protein 7g	0%

Per cent daily values are based on a 2000 calorie diet

STUFFED PASTA SHELLS

SERVES 4

These large pasta shells are ideal for filling and serving with a sauce. Quick to cook, they look fabulous and are great for entertaining.

16 large pasta shells

For the sauce

450 g (16 oz) can chopped tomatoes
2 garlic cloves, crushed
15 ml (1 tbsp) fresh chopped parsley
1 onion, chopped
2 tbsp tomato purée
ground black pepper

For the filling

60 ml (4 tbsp) vegetable stock
1 courgette, diced
40 g (1½ oz) canned or frozen corn
    kernels
1 green pepper, seeded and diced
50 g (2 oz) button mushrooms, sliced
1 leek, sliced
2 garlic cloves, crushed
15 g (1 tbsp) fresh chopped mixed
    herbs
basil sprigs to garnish

≈ Place the sauce ingredients in a pan, bring to the boil, cover, and simmer for 10 minutes. Transfer to a food processor and blend for 10 seconds. Return the sauce to the pan and heat through.
≈ Meanwhile, put all of the filling ingredients, except the herbs, in a saucepan and cook for 10 minutes, simmering until the vegetables are tender. Stir in the herbs and season.

≈ Cook the pasta in boiling salted water for 8–10 minutes until just tender, drain well. Spoon the vegetable filling into the pasta shells and arrange on warmed serving plates. Spoon the sauce around the shells, garnish with basil and serve.

WILD RICE AND LENTIL CASSEROLE

SERVES 4

This dish is superb on a cold day as it is really hearty and warming. To check that the rice is cooked, look at the ends to be sure they have split open, otherwise cook for a little longer until it is visibly cooked through.

≈ Cook the lentils and wild rice in the vegetable stock in a large flameproof casserole dish for 20 minutes, stirring occasionally.

≈ Add the onion, garlic, tomatoes, spices, mushrooms, pepper, broccoli and corn. Bring the mixture to the boil, reduce the heat and cook for a further 15 minutes until the rice and lentils are cooked. Add the chopped coriander, garnish and serve with warm crusty bread.

NUTRITION FACTS	
Serving Size 1 (251g)	
Calories 82	Calories from Fat 9
	% Daily Value
Total Fat 1g	2%
Saturated Fat 0g	1%
Monounsaturated Fat 0.19g	0%
Polyunsaturated Fat 0.3g	0%
Cholesterol 0mg	0%
Sodium 461mg	19%
Total Carbohydrate 18g	6%
Dietary Fibre 3g	13%
Sugars 7g	0%
Protein 3g	0%

Per cent daily values are based on a 2000 calorie diet

VEGETABLE FLAN

SERVES 4

This flan is made with a low-fat pastry which is flavoured with mustard. Although it is not quite as short as a traditional pastry it is delicious hot when filled with vegetables and low-fat cheese.

For the pastry

115 g (4 oz) flour

30 ml (2 tbsp) skimmed milk

75 g (1½ tsp) baking powder

5 g (1 tsp) mustard powder

For the filling

1 celery stick, sliced

50 g (2 oz) button mushrooms, sliced

2 baby corn cobs, sliced

1 leek, sliced

2 garlic cloves, crushed

8 asparagus spears, trimmed

125 ml (4 fl oz) vegetable stock

115 g (4 oz) low-fat cottage cheese

150 ml (¼ pint) skimmed milk

1 egg white, beaten

NUTRITION FACTS	
Serving Size 1 (256g)	
Calories 207	Calories from Fat 18
	% Daily Value
Total Fat 2g	3%
Saturated Fat 0g	2%
Monounsaturated Fat 0.2g	0%
Polyunsaturated Fat 0.3g	0%
Cholesterol 2mg	1%
Sodium 506mg	21%
Total Carbohydrate 37g	12%
Dietary Fibre 2g	7%
Sugars 6g	0%
Protein 12g	0%

Per cent daily values are based on a 2000 calorie diet

≈ Heat the oven to 200°C (400°F, Gas 6). Mix the pastry ingredients in a bowl and add enough cold water to bring the mixture together to form a soft dough. Roll the pastry out on a lightly floured surface to fit an 20 cm (8 in) pie dish.

≈ Cook the prepared vegetables in the stock for 5 minutes, stirring. Remove from the pan with a draining spoon and place in a bowl. Add the cottage cheese, milk and egg white. Spoon the mixture into the pastry case and cook for 40 minutes until set and golden brown. Serve hot with salad.

Wild Rice and Lentil Casserole

200 g (7 oz) red split lentils

50 g (2 oz) wild rice

1 litre (1¾ pints) vegetable stock

1 red onion, cut into eight pieces

2 garlic cloves, crushed

400 g (14 oz) can chopped tomatoes

5 g (1 tsp) ground coriander

5 g (1 tsp) ground cumin

5 g (1 tsp) chilli powder

salt and ground black pepper

200 g (7 oz) button mushrooms,
   sliced

1 green pepper, seeded and sliced

75 g (3 oz) broccoli florets

150 g (5 oz) baby corn cobs, halved

15 g (1 tbsp) fresh chopped
   coriander

coriander sprigs to garnish

NUTRITION FACTS	
Serving Size 1 (593g)	
Calories 242	Calories from Fat 27
	% Daily Value
Total Fat 3g	4%
Saturated Fat 0g	1%
Monounsaturated Fat 0.2g	0%
Polyunsaturated Fat 0.5g	0%
Cholesterol 0mg	0%
Sodium 1384mg	58%
Total Carbohydrate 43g	14%
Dietary Fibre 16g	66%
Sugars 7g	0%
Protein 10g	0%

Per cent daily values are based on a 2000 calorie diet

SPICY CHICK-PEAS

SERVES 4

Chick-peas are a great source of carbohydrate and are important in a vegetarian diet. Here they are simmered in a spicy tomato sauce and are delicious served with brown rice.

200 g (7 oz) chick-peas

5 g (1 tsp) bicarbonate of soda

1 onion, halved and sliced

2.5 cm (1 in) piece of root ginger, grated

4 tomatoes, chopped

1 green chilli, chopped

5 g (1 tsp) curry powder

2.5 g (½ tsp) chilli powder

5 g (1 tsp) ground coriander

300 ml (½ pint) vegetable stock

fresh chopped coriander to garnish

NUTRITION FACTS	
Serving Size 1 (274g)	
Calories 250 K Calories from Fat 36	
	% Daily Value
Total Fat 4g	6%
Saturated Fat 1g	5%
Monounsaturated Fat 1.4g	0%
Polyunsaturated Fat 0.9g	0%
Cholesterol 4mg	1%
Sodium 709mg	30%
Total Carbohydrate 42g	14%
Dietary Fibre 4g	15%
Sugars 7g	0%
Protein 14g	0%

Per cent daily values are based on a 2000 calorie diet

≈ Put the chick-peas in a large mixing bowl with the bicarbonate of soda and enough water to cover. Leave to soak overnight. Drain the chick-peas and cover with fresh water in a large saucepan. Bring to the boil and boil rapidly for 10 minutes. Reduce the heat and simmer for 1 hour or until cooked.

≈ Drain the chick-peas and put in a non-stick frying pan with the remaining ingredients. Cover and simmer for 20 minutes, stirring occasionally. Garnish with coriander and serve with brown rice.

WINTER VEGETABLE CASSEROLE

SERVES 4

This recipe makes use of many winter vegetables, but use whatever you have to hand as long as there is a good mixture. Cauliflower helps to thicken the sauce slightly, therefore it is always best to include this in your recipe.

2 large potatoes, sliced

900 ml (1½ pints) vegetable stock

2 carrots, cut into chunks

1 onion, sliced

2 garlic cloves, crushed

2 parsnips, cored and sliced

1 leek, sliced

2 celery sticks, sliced

175 g (6 oz) cauliflower florets

salt and ground black pepper

5 g (1 tsp) paprika

30 g (2 tbsp) fresh chopped mixed
    herbs

25 g (1 oz) low-fat vegetarian
    cheese, grated

≈ Cook the potatoes in boiling water for 10 minutes. Drain well and reserve. Meanwhile, heat 300 ml (½ pint) of the stock in a flameproof casserole dish. Add all of the vegetables, remaining stock, seasoning, and paprika and cook for 15 minutes stirring occasionally. Add the herbs and adjust the seasoning.

≈ Lay the potato slices on top of the vegetable mixture and sprinkle the cheese on top. Cook in the oven at 190°C (375°F, Gas 5) for 30 minutes or until the top is golden brown and the cheese has melted. Serve with a salad.

NUTRITION FACTS	
Serving Size 1 (479g)	
Calories 180	Calories from Fat 27
	% Daily Value
Total Fat 3g	5%
Saturated Fat 0g	1%
Monounsaturated Fat 0.8g	0%
Polyunsaturated Fat 0.5g	0%
Cholesterol 0mg	0%
Sodium 1520mg	63%
Total Carbohydrate 35g	12%
Dietary Fibre 5g	22%
Sugars 9g	0%
Protein 8g	0%

Per cent daily values are based on a 2000 calorie diet

ROAST PEPPER TART

SERVES 8

This is one of those dishes that is as appealing to the eye as to the palate. A medley of roast peppers in a cheese sauce are served in a crisp filo pastry case. For a dinner party, make individual pastry cases and serve the tarts with a small salad.

225 g (8 oz) filo pastry

225 g (8 oz) margarine, melted

For the filling

2 red peppers, seeded and halved

2 green peppers, seeded and halved

2 garlic cloves, crushed

For the sauce

300 ml (½ pint) skimmed milk

25 g (1 oz) low-fat vegetarian
    cheese, grated

30 g (2 tbsp) cornflour

50 ml (4 fl oz) vegetable stock

15 g (1 tbsp) fresh snipped chives

15 g (1 tbsp) fresh chopped basil

1 garlic clove, crushed

5 ml (1 tsp) wholegrain mustard

basil and chives to garnish

NUTRITION FACTS	
Serving Size 1 (150g)	
Calories 150	Calories from Fat 36
	% Daily Value
Total Fat 4g	6%
Saturated Fat 1g	3%
Monounsaturated Fat 1.4g	0%
Polyunsaturated Fat 1.5g	0%
Cholesterol 1mg	0%
Sodium 235mg	10%
Total Carbohydrate 23g	8%
Dietary Fibre 1g	2%
Sugars 2g	0%
Protein 5g	0%

Per cent daily values are based on a 2000 calorie diet

≈ Lay two sheets of filo pastry in a pie plate allowing the pastry to overhang the sides a little. Brush with margarine and lay another two sheets on top at opposite angles. Brush with margarine and continue in this way until all of the pastry has been used. Heat the oven to 200°C (400°F, Gas 6) and cook the pastry case for 15 minutes until golden and crisp.

≈ Meanwhile, lay the peppers on a baking sheet, skin side uppermost. Sprinkle the garlic over the peppers, cook in the oven for 20 minutes. Allow to cool slightly then peel the peppers, discarding the skin. Cut the peppers into strips and place in the pastry case.

≈ Heat the milk for the sauce in a pan, add the cheese and stir until melted. Blend the cornflour with 4 tablespoons cold water and stir into the sauce to form a paste. Bring to the boil, stirring until thickened and add the remaining ingredients with the stock. Spoon the sauce over the peppers, garnish with basil and chives and serve.

PASTA TIMBALE

SERVES 8

This is a really different way to serve pasta in a courgette-lined mould which is baked until set and served with a tomato sauce.

≈ Cut the courgettes into thin strips with a vegetable peeler and blanch in boiling water for 2–3 minutes. Refresh the courgettes under cold water, then put in a bowl and cover with cold water until required.

≈ Cook the pasta in boiling salted water for 8–10 minutes until just tender. Drain well and reserve.

≈ Heat the stock in a saucepan and cook the onions, garlic, carrot, corn and pepper for 5 minutes. Stir in the pasta, cheese, tomatoes, eggs and oregano, season well and cook for 3 minutes, stirring well.

≈ Line a 1.2 litre (2 pint) mould or round tin with the courgette strips, covering the base and sides and allowing the strips to overhang the sides. Spoon the pasta mixture into the mould and fold the courgette strips over the pasta to cover.

≈ Stand the mould in a roasting tin half filled with boiling water, cover, and cook in the oven at 180°C (350°F, Gas 4) for 30–40 minutes until set.

≈ Meanwhile, put all of the sauce ingredients in a pan and bring to the boil, reduce the heat and cook for 10 minutes. Sieve the sauce into a clean pan and heat gently.

≈ Remove the pasta dish from the oven and carefully turn out of the mould on to a serving plate. Serve with the tomato sauce.

2 courgettes

115 g (4 oz) pasta shapes such as macaroni or penne

90 ml (6 tbsp) vegetable stock

2 onions, chopped

2 garlic cloves, crushed

1 carrot, chopped

30 g (2 tbsp) drained, canned corn

1 green pepper, seeded and chopped

25 g (1 oz) low-fat vegetarian cheese, grated

450 g (16 oz) can chopped tomatoes

2 eggs, beaten

30 g (2 tbsp) fresh chopped oregano

For the sauce

1 onion, chopped

450 g (1 lb) tomatoes, chopped

10 g (2 tsp) granulated sugar

30 ml (2 tbsp) tomato purée

175 ml (6 fl oz) vegetable stock

NUTRITION FACTS	
Serving Size 1 (219g)	
Calories 100	Calories from Fat 27
	% Daily Value
Total Fat 3g	5%
Saturated Fat 1g	3%
Monounsaturated Fat 0.9g	0%
Polyunsaturated Fat 0.4g	0%
Cholesterol 58mg	19%
Sodium 451mg	19%
Total Carbohydrate 14g	5%
Dietary Fibre 2g	9%
Sugars 3g	0%
Protein 6g	0%

Per cent daily values are based on a 2000 calorie diet

SAFFRON RICE AND VEGETABLES

SERVES 4

Basmati rice is grown in the foothills of the Himalayas. It is a narrow long-grain white rice, and one of the best to accompany spicy dishes such as this recipe.

≈ Heat half of the stock for the rice in a saucepan and add the garlic, onion, rice and saffron. Cook for 4 minutes, stirring. Add the remaining ingredients for the rice and bring to the boil. Reduce the heat to a simmer and cook for a further 20–30 minutes until the rice is cooked.

≈ Meanwhile, put all of the ingredients for the vegetables, except the yogurt, in a large saucepan and cook for 20 minutes, stirring occasionally until the vegetables are tender. Remove from the heat and stir in the yogurt. Serve with the spicy rice and bread.

For the rice

600 ml (1 pint) vegetable stock
2 garlic cloves, crushed
1 onion, sliced
200 g (7 oz) basmati rice
a few strands of saffron
50 g (2 oz) frozen peas
4 cardamom pods
3 cloves
1 bay leaf
5 g (1 tsp) curry powder

For the vegetables

300 ml (1/2 pint) vegetable stock
1 onion, cut into eight pieces
3 garlic cloves
4 tomatoes, chopped
2 courgettes, sliced
1 potato, cubed
50 g (2 oz) French beans, trimmed
    and halved
5 g (1 tsp) curry powder
5 g (1 tsp) ground cumin
5 g (1 tsp) ground coriander
5 g (1 tsp) fennel seeds
150 ml (1/4 pint) low-fat natural
    yogurt

VEGETABLE PILAFF

SERVES 4

A pilaff is a spicy, fluffy rice. This recipe is packed with crisp vegetables, chestnuts and raisins and lightly coloured with saffron for a golden appearance. If you do not have saffron to hand, use a pinch of turmeric in its place.

≈ Heat the oil in a frying pan and add the onion and rice. Cook for 3–4 minutes, stirring. Add the remaining ingredients and bring the mixture to the boil. Reduce the heat and cook for a further 30 minutes, stirring occasionally until the rice is cooked and the liquid absorbed.

≈ Mix together the sauce ingredients and serve with the pilaff and a side salad.

NUTRITION FACTS	
Serving Size 1 (710g)	
Calories 521	Calories from Fat 63
	% Daily Value
Total Fat 7g	10%
Saturated Fat 0g	2%
Monounsaturated Fat 0.3g	0%
Polyunsaturated Fat 0.4g	0%
Cholesterol 2mg	1%
Sodium 1053mg	44%
Total Carbohydrate 109g	36%
Dietary Fibre 15g	60%
Sugars 14g	0%
Protein 14g	0%

Per cent daily values are based on a 2000 calorie diet

Vegetable Pilaff

30 ml (2 tbsp) sunflower oil

1 red onion, chopped

150 g (5 oz) basmati rice

a few strands of saffron

40 g (1½ oz) corn kernels

1 red pepper, seeded and diced

5 g (1 tsp) curry powder

5 g (1 tsp) chilli powder

1 green chilli, seeded and chopped

115 g (4 oz) broccoli florets

600 ml (1 pint) vegetable stock

115 g (4 oz) cooked and peeled
   chestnuts, halved

50 g (2 oz) raisins

For the sauce

150 ml (¼ pint) low-fat natural
   yogurt

30 g (2 tbsp) fresh chopped mint

a pinch of cayenne pepper

NUTRITION FACTS	
Serving Size 1 (390g)	
Calories 379	Calories from Fat 90
	% Daily Value
Total Fat 10g	15%
Saturated Fat 1g	6%
Monounsaturated Fat 3.4g	0%
Polyunsaturated Fat 3.0g	0%
Cholesterol 2mg	1%
Sodium 781mg	33%
Total Carbohydrate 69g	23%
Dietary Fibre 5g	20%
Sugars 21g	0%
Protein 9g	0%

Per cent daily values are based on a 2000 calorie diet

VEGETABLE RISOTTO

SERVES 4

R isotto is an Italian dish of cooked rice and either vegetables or meat. It has a creamy texture which is due to the special arborio risotto rice used. The recipe really does call for this but if you do not have any to hand it will still taste great with brown rice.

25 g (1½ tbsp) polyunsaturated margarine

1 onion, halved and sliced

225 g (8 oz) firm, lite tofu, cubed

225 g (8 oz) arborio rice

2.5 ml (½ tsp) turmeric

5 ml (1 tsp) soya sauce

600 ml (1 pint) vegetable stock

1 green chilli, sliced

1 red pepper, seeded, halved and sliced

50 g (2 oz) mangetout

75 g (3 oz) canned waterchestnuts, drained and halved

40 g (1½ oz) oyster mushrooms

NUTRITION FACTS	
Serving Size 1 (372g)	
Calories 182	Calories from Fat 54
	% Daily Value
Total Fat 6g	9%
Saturated Fat 1g	5%
Monounsaturated Fat 2.1g	0%
Polyunsaturated Fat 1.8g	0%
Cholesterol 0mg	0%
Sodium 911mg	38%
Total Carbohydrate 26g	9%
Dietary Fibre 1g	5%
Sugars 2g	0%
Protein 8g	0%

Per cent daily values are based on a 2000 calorie diet

≈ Heat the margarine in a non-stick frying pan and cook the onion and tofu for 3 minutes. Add the rice and turmeric and cook for a further 2 minutes.

≈ Add the soya sauce to the pan with the stock, chilli, pepper, mangetout and waterchestnuts. Bring the mixture to the boil, reduce the heat to a simmer and cook for 15–20 minutes until all of the vegetables are tender. Top the pan up with hot water or stock if required and stir frequently. Stir in the mushrooms and cook for 5 minutes and serve.

VEGETABLE CHOP SUEY

SERVES 4

A dd a touch of China to your table with this simple recipe. Vegetables are cooked in a spiced soya sauce and served with brown rice for a quick and healthy meal.

≈ Pour the vegetable stock into a large frying pan or wok with the Chinese five spice powder and cook all of the vegetables except the mushrooms and beansprouts for 5 minutes.

≈ Add the mushrooms, bean sprouts and soya sauce to the pan and cook for a further 5 minutes, stirring well. Serve immediately with boiled brown rice.

TOFU BURGERS AND CHIPS

SERVES 4

H ere is a recipe that low-fat dieters dream of. Although not chips in the strictest sense, these blanched potato sticks are tossed in flour and a little oil and baked to crispness in the oven.

≈ Boil the carrots in water for 10–12 minutes until soft. Drain really well. Cook the cabbage in boiling water for 5 minutes and drain really well. Put the carrots, cabbage, onion, tofu and coriander in a food processor and blend for 10 seconds. Using floured hands form the mixture into four equal-sized burgers. Chill in the refrigerator for 1 hour or until firm.

≈ Cut the potatoes into thick chips and cook in boiling water for 10 minutes. Drain well and toss in the flour. Put the potatoes in a plastic bag and sprinkle in the oil. Seal the top of the bag and shake the fries to coat. Turn the potatoes out on to a non-stick baking sheet. Cook in the oven at 200°C (400°F, Gas 6) for 30 minutes or until golden brown.

≈ Meanwhile, place the burgers under a hot grill for 7–8 minutes, turning with a fish slice. Toast the burger buns for 2 minutes and place a burger on one half. Add the tomatoes, lettuce and onion and serve with the chips.

---

300 ml (1/2 pint) vegetable stock

5 g (1 tsp) Chinese five spice powder

3 carrots, cut into strips

3 celery sticks, sliced

1 red onion, sliced

1 green pepper, seeded and cut into chunks

40 g (1 1/2 oz) open cap mushrooms, sliced

225 g (8 oz) bean sprouts

15 ml (1 tbsp) light soya sauce

NUTRITION FACTS

Serving Size 1 (250g)

Calories 57	Calories from Fat 9
	% Daily Value

Total Fat 1g	1%
Saturated Fat 0g	0%
Monounsaturated Fat 0.1g	0%
Polyunsaturated Fat 0.3g	0%
Cholesterol 0mg	0%
Sodium 620mg	26%
Total Carbohydrate 10g	3%
Dietary Fibre 3g	10%
Sugars 4g	0%
Protein 4g	0%

Per cent daily values are based on a 2000 calorie diet

For the burgers

185 g (6 1/2 oz) carrots, chopped

50 g (2 oz) cabbage, shredded

1 onion, chopped

275 g (10 oz) firm, lite tofu, cubed

5 g (1 tsp) ground coriander

4 burger buns split

sliced tomatoes, lettuce and onion

For the fries

2 large potatoes

30 g (2 tbsp) flour

15 ml (1 tbsp) sunflower oil

NUTRITION FACTS

Serving Size 1 (459g)

Calories 280	Calories from Fat 63
	% Daily Value

Total Fat 7g	11%
Saturated Fat 1g	5%
Monounsaturated Fat 2.0g	0%
Polyunsaturated Fat 3.0g	0%
Cholesterol 0mg	0%
Sodium 218mg	9%
Total Carbohydrate 38g	13%
Dietary Fibre 5g	20%
Sugars 8g	0%
Protein 17g	0%

Per cent daily values are based on a 2000 calorie diet

SEASONAL SIDE-DISH SELECTION

Trio of Purées

Potato and Cheese Layer

Herbed Cauliflower

Paprika Potato Salad

Stuffed Peppers

Minted Beans and Cucumber

Chestnut Brown Rice

Vegetable Gratinée

Spiced Aubergines

Steamed Honey-glazed Parsnips

Mixed Vegetable Dumplings

Sweet Red Cabbage

Caramelized Baked Onions

Hot Spicy Lentils

Three-Mushroom Fry

Ratatouille

Herb Gnocchi

Quick Spiced Rice

TRIO OF PURÉES

SERVES 4

These colourful vegetable purée moulds are perfect for dinner parties. Alternatively, bake in one large ovenproof dish instead of individual moulds.

275 g (10 oz) potatoes, cubed

185 g (6½ oz) carrots, cubed

grated zest of 1 orange

15 ml (1 tbsp) orange juice

ground black pepper

225 g (8 oz) sweet potato, cubed

dash of grated nutmeg

115 g (4 oz) spinach

grated zest of 1 lemon

15 g (1 tbsp) fresh chopped coriander

NUTRITION FACTS

Serving Size 1 (189g)

Calories 154	Calories from Fat 0
	% Daily Value
Total Fat 0g	1%
Saturated Fat 0g	0%
Monounsaturated Fat 0g	0%
Polyunsaturated Fat 0.1g	0%
Cholesterol 0mg	0%
Sodium 55mg	2%
Total Carbohydrate 35g	12%
Dietary Fibre 7g	27%
Sugars 10g	0%
Protein 4g	0%

Per cent daily values are based on a 2000 calorie diet

≈ Cook the potatoes in boiling water for 20 minutes until soft. Drain and mash. Divide equally into three separate bowls.

≈ Boil the carrots for 10 minutes until soft. Drain and mash. Add to one bowl of potato with the orange zest and juice. Season with pepper.

≈ Cook the sweet potato for 10 minutes in boiling water. Drain and mash. Add to another bowl of potato with the nutmeg. Season with pepper.

≈ Blanch the spinach for 3 minutes in boiling water. Drain very well, pressing out all the moisture through a sieve. Add to the remaining bowl with the lemon zest and coriander. Season with pepper.

≈ Place the contents of each bowl, separately, in a food processor and blend each for 1 minute. Repeat with each mixture. Spoon one-quarter of the carrot purée into the base of four lightly greased individual ramekin dishes. Top with one-quarter of the spinach mixture and finally spoon on one-quarter of the sweet potato mixture.

≈ Place the dishes in a roasting pan and fill with enough boiling water to come halfway up the sides. Cover and cook in the oven at 190°C (375°F, Gas 5) for 1 hour. Remove the ramekins from the roasting pan. Turn out the purées on to serving plates. Serve with a main vegetable dish.

POTATO AND CHEESE LAYER

SERVES 4

This recipe uses half fat cream substitute in place of full fat cream. If preferred, substitute with skimmed milk or vegetable stock.

450 g (1 lb) potatoes, thinly sliced

2 garlic cloves, crushed

50 g (2 oz) low-fat cheese, grated

1 onion, halved and sliced

30 g (2 tbsp) fresh chopped parsley

125 ml (4 fl oz) half cream substitute

25 ml (4 fl oz) skimmed milk

ground black pepper

fresh chopped parsley to garnish

NUTRITION FACTS

Serving Size 1 (179g)

Calories 159	Calories from Fat 9
	% Daily Value
Total Fat 1g	2%
Saturated Fat 0g	2%
Monounsaturated Fat 0.6g	0%
Polyunsaturated Fat 0.2g	0%
Cholesterol 1mg	0%
Sodium 44mg	2%
Total Carbohydrate 34g	11%
Dietary Fibre 3g	12%
Sugars 3g	0%
Protein 4g	0%

Per cent daily values are based on a 2000 calorie diet

≈ Cook the potatoes in boiling water for 10 minutes. Drain well. Arrange a layer of potatoes in the base of a shallow ovenproof dish. Add a little garlic, cheese, onion and parsley. Repeat the layers until all the potatoes, onion, cheese, garlic and parsley are used, finishing with a layer of cheese.

≈ Mix together the half cream substitute and milk. Season and pour over the potato layers. Bake in the oven at 160°C (325°F, Gas 3) for 1¼ hours until cooked through and golden brown. Garnish with parsley and serve.

Potato and Cheese Layer ▶

HERBED CAULIFLOWER

SERVES 4

Cauliflower cheese traditionally has a rich cheese sauce coating the cauliflower. This low-fat version uses a wine and herb sauce which is equally delicious.

4 baby cauliflowers

2 mint sprigs

900 ml (1½ pints) vegetable stock

25 g (1 oz) low-fat cheese, grated

For the sauce

150 ml (¼ pint) vegetable stock

300 ml (½ pint) skimmed milk

150 ml (¼ pint) dry white wine

30 g (2 tbsp) cornflour

15 g (1 tbsp) fresh chopped parsley

15 g (1 tbsp) fresh chopped
   coriander

15 g (1 tbsp) fresh chopped thyme

ground black pepper

NUTRITION FACTS	
Serving Size 1 (846g)	
Calories 160	Calories from Fat 27
	% Daily Value
Total Fat 3g	4%
Saturated Fat 0g	2%
Monounsaturated Fat 0.1g	0%
Polyunsaturated Fat 0.0g	0%
Cholesterol 4mg	1%
Sodium 1309mg	55%
Total Carbohydrate 24g	8%
Dietary Fibre 12g	46%
Sugars 18g	0%
Protein 16g	0%

Per cent daily values are based on a 2000 calorie diet

≈ Trim the cauliflowers and place in a large pan with the mint and stock. Cook gently for 10 minutes.

≈ Meanwhile, place the stock for the sauce, the milk and white wine in a pan. Blend the cornflour with 60 ml (4 tablespoons) of cold water and add to the pan. Bring to the boil, stirring, and add the herbs. Season and simmer for 2–3 minutes.

≈ Drain the cauliflower and place in an ovenproof dish. Pour on the sauce and top with the cheese. Grill for 2–3 minutes until the cheese has melted. Serve.

PAPRIKA POTATO SALAD

SERVES 4

This salad has a spicy Indian flavour. Perfect served accompanying either a spiced main dish or a green salad.

450 g (1 lb) potatoes

125 ml (4 fl oz) vegetable stock

1 red onion, halved and sliced

1.5 g (¼ tsp) ground cumin

1 green chilli, chopped

1.5 g (¼ tsp) ground turmeric

1 cardamom pod

5 g (1 tsp) paprika

1 tomato, seeded and diced

15 g (1 tbsp) fresh chopped parsley

≈ Cut the potatoes into 2.5 cm (1 in) cubes. Cook in boiling water for 10 minutes. Drain well and reserve.

≈ Heat 45 ml (3 tablespoons) of the stock in a pan, add the onion and cook for 5 minutes until beginning to brown. Add the potatoes, cumin, chilli, turmeric, cardamom pod and paprika. Stir in the remaining stock and the tomato. Bring to the boil and cook for 5 minutes. Sprinkle with parsley and serve.

NUTRITION FACTS	
Serving Size 1 (219g)	
Calories 159	Calories from Fat 9
	% Daily Value
Total Fat 1g	1%
Saturated Fat 0g	0%
Monounsaturated Fat 0.0g	0%
Polyunsaturated Fat 0.2g	0%
Cholesterol 0mg	0%
Sodium 199mg	8%
Total Carbohydrate 35g	12%
Dietary Fibre 5g	22%
Sugars 4g	0%
Protein 4g	0%

Per cent daily values are based on a 2000 calorie diet

STUFFED PEPPERS

SERVES 4

These peppers are filled with bulgur wheat flavoured with cheese, vegetables and fruit. Serve as an accompaniment or as a meal in themselves.

115 g (4 oz) bulgur wheat
250 ml (8 fl oz) vegetable stock
4 red peppers
1.5 g (¼ tsp) ground turmeric
40 g (1½ oz) mushrooms, diced
30 g (2 tbsp) raisins
30 g (2 tbsp) dried apricots, diced
3 spring onions, sliced
25 g (1 oz) low-fat cheese, grated
30 g (2 tbsp) fresh chopped coriander
1.5 g (¼ tsp) cayenne pepper
ground black pepper

≈ Place the bulgur wheat in a bowl and pour on the vegetable stock. Stand for 30 minutes. Drain if required.
≈ Meanwhile, cut the tops from the peppers and remove the core and seeds. Cook the peppers in boiling water for 2 minutes, drain and refresh under cold water.

≈ Mix together the remaining ingredients. Stir into the bulgur wheat and spoon into the peppers. Season with black pepper.
≈ Stand the peppers in a shallow oven-proof dish and pour in enough boiling water to come halfway up the sides. Cover and cook in the oven at 180°C (350°F, Gas 4) for 20 minutes. Serve.

NUTRITION FACTS

Serving Size 1 (268g)

Calories 209	Calories from Fat 9

	% Daily Value
Total Fat 1g	2%
Saturated Fat 0g	1%
Monounsaturated Fat 0.1g	0%
Polyunsaturated Fat 0.2g	0%
Cholesterol 2mg	1%
Sodium 274mg	11%
Total Carbohydrate 44g	15%
Dietary Fibre 8g	32%
Sugars 3g	0%
Protein 8g	0%

Per cent daily values are based on a 2000 calorie diet

MINTED BEANS AND CUCUMBER

SERVES 4

Cucumber is not usually served hot, but it is cooked perfectly with the beans in this recipe and delicately flavoured with mint. An unusual but delicious side dish.

450 g (1 lb) French beans, trimmed
½ cucumber, thickly sliced
2 garlic cloves, crushed
4 mint sprigs
15 ml (1 tbsp) lemon juice
75 ml (3 fl oz) vegetable stock
ground black pepper
strips of lemon zest for garnish

≈ Prepare the vegetables and place on a large sheet of foil. Bring up the sides of the foil around the vegetables and crimp to form an open parcel. Add the remaining ingredients, season and seal the top of the parcel.

≈ Place the parcel in a steamer and cook for 25 minutes or until the beans are tender. Garnish and serve.

NUTRITION FACTS

Serving Size 1 (185g)

Calories 40	Calories from Fat 9

	% Daily Value
Total Fat 1g	2%
Saturated Fat 0g	1%
Monounsaturated Fat 0.4g	0%
Polyunsaturated Fat 0.3g	0%
Cholesterol 0mg	0%
Sodium 106mg	4%
Total Carbohydrate 6g	2%
Dietary Fibre 2g	9%
Sugars 3g	0%
Protein 2g	0%

Per cent daily values are based on a 2000 calorie diet

Minted Beans and Cucumber ▶

CHESTNUT BROWN RICE

SERVES 4

Chestnuts are one of the few nuts that are not very high in fat. They add to the nutty flavour of the rice in this recipe.

900 ml (1½ pints) vegetable stock

200 g (7 oz) brown rice

1 red onion, halved and sliced

2 garlic cloves, crushed

115 g (4 oz) cooked chestnuts, quartered

2 celery sticks, sliced

45 g (3 tbsp) fresh chopped parsley

150 g (5 oz) corn kernels

ground black pepper

≈ Heat the vegetable stock in a pan, add the rice and onion and cook for 10 minutes.

≈ Stir in the garlic, chestnuts, celery, parsley and corn. Season well and cook for 40 minutes over a low heat until the rice is cooked and the liquid has been absorbed.

NUTRITION FACTS

Serving Size 1 (148g)

Calories 155	Calories from Fat 9
	% Daily Value
Total Fat 1g	2%
Saturated Fat 0g	1%
Monounsaturated Fat 0.4g	0%
Polyunsaturated Fat 0.4g	0%
Cholesterol 0mg	0%
Sodium 181mg	8%
Total Carbohydrate 34g	11%
Dietary Fibre 2g	8%
Sugars 5g	0%
Protein 4g	0%

Per cent daily values are based on a 2000 calorie diet

VEGETABLE GRATINÉE

SERVES 4

This colourful combination of baked vegetables is topped with breadcrumbs, coriander and cheese for added flavour and texture. It would make a perfect side dish or a light meal.

2 leeks, cut into strips lengthways

2 carrots, cut into sticks

75 g (3 oz) mangetout

175 g (6 oz) baby corn, halved

2 garlic cloves, crushed

15 ml (1 tbsp) clear honey

2.5 g (½ tsp) ground ginger

1.5 g (¼ tsp) grated nutmeg

150 ml (¼ pint) apple juice

150 ml (¼ pint) vegetable stock

50 g (2 oz) fresh white breadcrumbs

30 g (2 tbsp) fresh chopped coriander

25 g (1 oz) low-fat cheese, grated

≈ Place the vegetables in a large pan of boiling water and cook for 10 minutes. Drain well and place in a shallow oven-proof dish.

≈ Mix together the garlic, honey, ginger, nutmeg, apple juice and stock, and pour over the vegetables.

≈ Mix together the breadcrumbs and coriander. Sprinkle over the vegetables to cover. Top with the cheese. Bake in the oven at 200°C (400°F, Gas 6) for 45 minutes or until golden brown. Serve.

NUTRITION FACTS

Serving Size 1 (243g)

Calories 164	Calories from Fat 18
	% Daily Value
Total Fat 2g	3%
Saturated Fat 0g	2%
Monounsaturated Fat 0.4g	0%
Polyunsaturated Fat 0.4g	0%
Cholesterol 2mg	1%
Sodium 363mg	15%
Total Carbohydrate 34g	11%
Dietary Fibre 3g	12%
Sugars 13g	0%
Protein 6g	0%

Per cent daily values are based on a 2000 calorie diet

Vegetable Gratinée ▶

SPICED AUBERGINES

SERVES 4

An Indian aubergine dish which is perfect with curry or a plain vegetable casserole. Spicy in itself, it is also delicious cold as an appetizer.

450 g (1 lb) aubergines

175 g (6 oz) potatoes

60 ml (4 tbsp) vegetable stock

½ onion, sliced

1 small red pepper, seeded and diced

1.5 g (¼ tsp) ground coriander

1.5 g (¼ tsp) ground cumin

5 g (1 tsp) root ginger, grated

2.5 g (½ tsp) curry powder

3 garlic cloves, crushed

5 g (1 tsp) chilli powder

dash of ground turmeric

dash of sugar

1 green chilli, diced

15 g (1 tbsp) fresh chopped coriander

NUTRITION FACTS	
Serving Size 1 (206g)	
Calories 110	Calories from Fat 9
	% Daily Value
Total Fat 1g	1%
Saturated Fat 0g	0%
Monounsaturated Fat 0.0g	0%
Polyunsaturated Fat 0.1g	0%
Cholesterol 0mg	0%
Sodium 78mg	3%
Total Carbohydrate 25g	8%
Dietary Fibre 5g	20%
Sugars 3g	0%
Protein 3g	0%

Per cent daily values are based on a 2000 calorie diet

≈ Dice the aubergines into small cubes. Cut the potatoes into 2.5 cm (1 in) chunks.
≈ Heat the stock in a pan, add the onion and cook for 2–3 minutes. Stir in the red pepper, ground coriander, cumin, ginger, curry powder, garlic, chilli powder and turmeric, and cook for 2–3 minutes.

≈ Add the aubergine, sugar, green chilli and 150 ml (¼ pint) water, cover and simmer for 15 minutes. Add the potato, re-cover and cook for 10 minutes. Stir in the fresh coriander and serve.

86

STEAMED HONEY-GLAZED PARSNIPS

SERVES 4

Traditionally parsnips are roasted or baked, but they steam equally well and in far less time.

≈ Cook the parsnips in boiling water for 5 minutes. Drain well and place in a steamer lined with foil.

≈ Mix together the honey, ginger, cumin seeds, vegetable stock and coriander. Pour over the parsnips and season.

≈ Cover and steam for 20 minutes or until cooked through. Serve immediately with the cooking liquid.

8 baby parsnips
30 ml (2 tbsp) honey
2.5 g (½ tsp) ground ginger
2.5 g (½ tsp) cumin seeds
125 ml (4 fl oz) vegetable stock
15 g (1 tbsp) fresh chopped coriander
ground black pepper

NUTRITION FACTS	
Serving Size 1 (100g)	
Calories 90	Calories from Fat 0
	% Daily Value
Total Fat 0g	1%
Saturated Fat 0g	0%
Monounsaturated Fat 0.1g	0%
Polyunsaturated Fat 0.0g	0%
Cholesterol 0mg	0%
Sodium 80mg	3%
Total Carbohydrate 22g	7%
Dietary Fibre 3g	13%
Sugars 9g	0%
Protein 2g	0%

Per cent daily values are based on a 2000 calorie diet

MIXED VEGETABLE DUMPLINGS

MAKES 24

These are like Chinese dumplings or Dim Sum. A water and flour dough encases delicately chopped vegetables. Quickly steamed they are perfect with a Chinese main course.

≈ Mix all the filling ingredients together in a bowl.

≈ Place 275 g (10 oz) of the flour for the dough in a bowl. Stir in 125 ml (4 fl oz) boiling water, 60 ml (4 tablespoons) cold water and the oil. Bring the mixture together to form a dough. Sprinkle the remaining flour on a work surface and knead the dough until smooth. Roll the dough into a long sausage shape and cut into 24 equal pieces. Roll each piece into a 5 cm (2 in) round.

≈ Divide the filling into 24 and spoon into the centre of each round. Bring the edges of the dough together in the centre and pinch together to seal as a parcel.

≈ Line a steamer with a damp cloth, place one-quarter of the dumplings in the steamer and steam for 5 minutes. Repeat with the remaining dumplings and serve.

For the filling

1 small carrot, finely chopped
1 celery stick, chopped
1 spring onion, chopped
1 small courgette, finely chopped
2 garlic cloves, crushed
7.5 ml (½ tbsp) soya sauce
dash of sugar
5 ml (1 tsp) dry sherry
15 g (1 tbsp) cornflour

For the dough

350 g (12 oz) plain flour
15 ml (1 tbsp) polyunsaturated oil

NUTRITION FACTS	
Serving Size 1 (29g)	
Calories 68	Calories from Fat 9
	% Daily Value
Total Fat 1g	1%
Saturated Fat 0g	0%
Monounsaturated Fat 0.0g	0%
Polyunsaturated Fat 0.4g	0%
Cholesterol 0mg	0%
Sodium 25mg	1%
Total Carbohydrate 13g	4%
Dietary Fibre 1g	3%
Sugars 1g	0%
Protein 2g	0%

Per cent daily values are based on a 2000 calorie diet

SWEET RED CABBAGE

SERVES 4

Colourful and with a sweet and sour flavour, it may also be served cold.

300 ml (½ pint) vegetable stock

675 g (1½ lb) red cabbage, cored and shredded

1 onion, sliced

15 g (1 tbsp) soft brown sugar

5 g (1 tsp) ground allspice

225 g (8 oz) green apples, cored and sliced

5 g (1 tsp) fennel seeds

30 ml (2 tbsp) cider vinegar

15 g (1 tbsp) cornflour

15 g (1 tbsp) fresh chopped parsley

NUTRITION FACTS	
Serving Size 1 (328g)	
Calories 106	Calories from Fat 9
	% Daily Value
Total Fat 1g	1%
Saturated Fat 0g	1%
Monounsaturated Fat 0.0g	0%
Polyunsaturated Fat 0.3g	0%
Cholesterol 0mg	0%
Sodium 178mg	7%
Total Carbohydrate 24g	8%
Dietary Fibre 3g	13%
Sugars 11g	0%
Protein 3g	0%

Per cent daily values are based on a 2000 calorie diet

≈ Place half of the stock in a large saucepan. Add the cabbage and onion and cook over a high heat for 5 minutes. ≈ Add the sugar, allspice, apples, fennel seeds, vinegar and remaining stock. Blend the cornflour with 30 ml (2 tablespoons) of cold water to form a paste. Stir into the pan and bring to the boil, stirring until thickened and clear.

≈ Reduce the heat and cook for a further 15 minutes until the cabbage is cooked. Sprinkle with the parsley and serve.

CARAMELIZED BAKED ONIONS

SERVES 4

These baked onions have a slightly "burnt" taste which complements the sweetness of the onion. Serve with a simple main dish.

4 large onions

10 g (2 tsp) polyunsaturated margarine

75 g (tbsp) soft brown sugar

NUTRITION FACTS	
Serving Size 1 (10g)	
Calories 31	Calories from Fat 9
	% Daily Value
Total Fat 1g	1%
Saturated Fat 0g	1%
Monounsaturated Fat 0.4g	0%
Polyunsaturated Fat 0.3g	0%
Cholesterol 0mg	0%
Sodium 3mg	0%
Total Carbohydrate 6g	2%
Dietary Fibre 0g	0%
Sugars 0g	0%
Protein 0g	0%

Per cent daily values are based on a 2000 calorie diet

≈ Cut the onions into quarters and then into four again. Cook in boiling water for 10 minutes. Drain well.

≈ Place the margarine and sugar in a pan and heat gently until melted. Place the onions in a roasting tin and pour over the margarine and sugar. Cook in the oven at 190°C (375°F, Gas 5) for 10 minutes until browned. Serve immediately.

Sweet Red Cabbage ▶

HOT SPICY LENTILS

SERVES 4

An example of using lentils in place of meat, this recipe can be eaten as a side dish or as a vegetarian meal.

175 g (6 oz) red lentils

20 ml (4 tsp) polyunsaturated oil

1 red onion, chopped

2 garlic cloves, crushed

1.5 g (¼ tsp) ground cumin

1.5 g (¼ tsp) ground coriander

1 red chilli, chopped

900 ml (1½ pints) vegetable stock

juice and grated zest of 1 lime

ground black pepper

≈ Wash the lentils in 2–3 changes of water. Drain and reserve. Heat the oil in a pan, add the onion, garlic, and spices and cook for 5 minutes. Stir in the lentils and cook for a further 3–4 minutes.

≈ Add the chilli and stock and bring to the boil. Reduce the heat and simmer gently for 35 minutes until the lentils are soft. Stir in the lime juice and rind. Season well and serve.

NUTRITION FACTS

Serving Size 1 (237g)

Calories 186	Calories from Fat 45
	% Daily Value
Total Fat 5g	8%
Saturated Fat 0g	2%
Monounsaturated Fat 0.6g	0%
Polyunsaturated Fat 3.5g	0%
Cholesterol 0mg	0%
Sodium 59mg	2%
Total Carbohydrate 23g	8%
Dietary Fibre 12g	46%
Sugars 0g	0%
Protein 14g	0%

Per cent daily values are based on a 2000 calorie diet

THREE-MUSHROOM FRY

SERVES 4

This really is a simple yet delicious dish. Three varieties of mushroom are cooked in garlic and soya sauce.

40 g (1½ oz) open cap mushrooms

75 g (3 oz) oyster mushrooms

50 g (2 oz) shiitake mushrooms

60 ml (4 tbsp) vegetable stock

2 garlic cloves, crushed

15 ml (1 tbsp) soya sauce

30 g (2 tbsp) fresh chopped parsley
or thyme

ground black pepper

≈ Peel the open cap mushrooms and thinly slice. Place all the mushrooms in a frying pan with the stock, garlic, soya sauce and half of the herbs. Season well with black pepper. Cook, stirring, for 3–4 minutes. Sprinkle in the remaining herbs and serve immediately.

NUTRITION FACTS

Serving Size 1 (129g)

Calories 71	Calories from Fat 0
	% Daily Value
Total Fat 0g	1%
Saturated Fat 0g	1%
Monounsaturated Fat 0.1g	0%
Polyunsaturated Fat 0.0g	0%
Cholesterol 0mg	0%
Sodium 289mg	12%
Total Carbohydrate 18g	6%
Dietary Fibre 3g	12%
Sugars 0g	0%
Protein 2g	0%

Per cent daily values are based on a 2000 calorie diet

Three-Mushroom Fry ▶

RATATOUILLE

SERVES 4

A medley of vegetables cooked in a tomato and herb sauce. This is a strongly flavoured dish to be served with a plainer recipe or used to top a jacket potato.

1 onion, halved and sliced

2 garlic cloves, crushed

150 ml (¼ pint) vegetable stock

1 large aubergine, sliced

175 g (6 oz) courgettes, sliced

1 green pepper, seeded and sliced

30 ml (2 tbsp) tomato purée

400 g (14 oz) can chopped tomatoes

30 g (2 tbsp) fresh chopped oregano

ground black pepper

NUTRITION FACTS	
Serving Size 1 (351g)	
Calories 83	Calories from Fat 9
	% Daily Value
Total Fat 1g	1%
Saturated Fat 0g	0%
Monounsaturated Fat 0.0g	0%
Polyunsaturated Fat 0.1g	0%
Cholesterol 0mg	0%
Sodium 228mg	10%
Total Carbohydrate 17g	6%
Dietary Fibre 3g	12%
Sugars 2g	0%
Protein 4g	0%

Per cent daily values are based on a 2000 calorie diet

≈ Place the onion, garlic, and stock in a frying pan and cook for 5 minutes until the onion softens. Add the aubergine, courgettes and yellow pepper and cook for a further 5 minutes.

≈ Stir in the tomato purée, chopped tomatoes and 15 g (1 tablespoon) of the oregano. Season well. Bring to the boil, cover and reduce the heat. Cook for 1 hour, stirring occasionally. Sprinkle with the remaining oregano and serve.

HERB GNOCCHI

SERVES 4

An Italian favourite, gnocchi can be made from potato, flour or a mixture of the two. They may be boiled, baked or grilled for a traditional accompaniment.

≈ Place the milk and stock in a saucepan and bring to the boil. Add to the cooked potato, with the coriander, egg white, margarine and 50 g (2 oz) of the cheese, stirring well.

≈ Spread the mixture into a shallow, lightly greased ovenproof dish and allow to cool. Sprinkle on the remaining cheese and grill for 5 minutes. Cut into squares and serve.

60 ml (4 tbsp) skimmed milk

60 ml (4 tbsp) vegetable stock

675 g (1½ lb) cooked potato, mashed ground black pepper

1.5 g (¼ tsp) ground coriander

1 egg white, beaten

30 g (2 tbsp) polyunsaturated margarine

75 g (3 oz) low-fat cheese, grated

NUTRITION FACTS	
Serving Size 1 (144g)	
Calories 165	Calories from Fat 36
	% Daily Value
Total Fat 4g	6%
Saturated Fat 1g	4%
Monounsaturated Fat 1.7g	0%
Polyunsaturated Fat 1.2g	0%
Cholesterol 0mg	0%
Sodium 109mg	5%
Total Carbohydrate 30g	10%
Dietary Fibre 3g	11%
Sugars 2g	0%
Protein 4g	0%

Per cent daily values are based on a 2000 calorie diet

QUICK SPICED RICE

SERVES 4

Unlike a risotto, the rice in this recipe is cooked separately and stirred into the vegetables at the end of cooking. This halves the cooking time to give a speedy vegetable meal or side dish.

≈ Place the stock in a frying pan, add the beans, corn, jalapeño chilli, tomatoes, celery, garlic and onion. Cook for 7 minutes, stirring. Add the asparagus, cayenne pepper and chilli powder and cook for a further 3 minutes.

≈ Meanwhile, cook the rice in boiling water and drain well. Stir the rice into the pan with the vegetables. Sprinkle with parsley and serve.

300 ml (½ pint) vegetable stock

225 g (8 oz) French beans, trimmed

150 g (5 oz) corn kernels

1 pickled jalapeño chilli, sliced

50 g (2 oz) sundried tomatoes, soaked in water overnight and sliced

2 celery sticks, sliced

3 garlic cloves, crushed

1 red onion, diced

4 asparagus spears, sliced

1.5 g (¼ tsp) cayenne pepper

1.5 g (¼ tsp) chilli powder

200 g (7 oz) long-grain brown rice

15 g (1 tbsp) fresh chopped parsley

NUTRITION FACTS	
Serving Size 1 (274g)	
Calories 157	Calories from Fat 18
	% Daily Value
Total Fat 2g	3%
Saturated Fat 0g	2%
Monounsaturated Fat 0.4g	0%
Polyunsaturated Fat 0.6g	0%
Cholesterol 0mg	0%
Sodium 608mg	25%
Total Carbohydrate 32g	11%
Dietary Fibre 6g	23%
Sugars 3g	0%
Protein 7g	0%

Per cent daily values are based on a 2000 calorie diet

DELICATE DESSERTS

Honeyed Oranges

Strawberry Fool

Apricot Sorbet

Melon Ice

Fruditées

Blueberry Crush

Apple Crumble Pie

Banana Ice Cream

Vanilla Mousse

Blueberry Cheesecake

Crème Caramel

Plum and Ginger Brûlée

Cappuccino Sponges

Cinnamon Toasts

Baked Apples

Poached Pears

HONEYED ORANGES

SERVES 4

Oranges and ginger make a great combination. Ground ginger has been added to this recipe with a dash of orange liqueur for extra flavour.

≈ Place the honey, cinnamon, ginger and mint in a pan with 150 ml (¼ pint) water. Heat gently to melt the honey. Bring to the boil and boil for 3 minutes to reduce by half. Remove the mint from the pan and discard. Stir in the Grand Marnier.

≈ Meanwhile, peel the oranges, remove the pith and slice thinly. Place the orange slices in a serving bowl, pour over the syrup and chill for 1 hour before serving.

60 ml (4 tbsp) honey

2.5 g (½ tsp) ground cinnamon

1.5 g (¼ tsp) ground ginger

2 mint sprigs

10 ml (2 tsp) Grand Marnier

4 oranges

NUTRITION FACTS	
Serving Size 1 (253g)	
Calories 141	Calories from Fat 0
	% Daily Value
Total Fat 0g	1%
Saturated Fat 0g	0%
Monounsaturated Fat 0.0g	0%
Polyunsaturated Fat 0.0g	0%
Cholesterol 0mg	0%
Sodium 4mg	0%
Total Carbohydrate 34g	11%
Dietary Fibre 10g	40%
Sugars 37g	0%
Protein 2g	0%

Per cent daily values are based on a 2000 calorie diet

STRAWBERRY FOOL

SERVES 4

This dish is simple to prepare, but should be made in advance of a meal as it requires chilling for 1 hour before serving.

≈ Place the chopped strawberries in a food processor with the icing sugar. Liquidize for 30 seconds until smooth.

≈ Place the yogurt in a bowl and stir in the strawberry mixture. Whisk the egg whites until peaks form and fold in gently. Spoon into serving glasses and chill for 1 hour. Decorate and serve.

275 g (10 oz) strawberries, hulled and chopped

50 g (2 oz) icing sugar

300 ml (½ pint) low-fat natural yogurt

2 egg whites

strawberry slices and mint sprigs to decorate

NUTRITION FACTS	
Serving Size 1 (181g)	
Calories 136	Calories from Fat 9
	% Daily Value
Total Fat 1g	2%
Saturated Fat 1g	4%
Monounsaturated Fat 0.3g	0%
Polyunsaturated Fat 0.1g	0%
Cholesterol 4mg	1%
Sodium 79mg	3%
Total Carbohydrate 25g	8%
Dietary Fibre 2g	7%
Sugars 8g	0%
Protein 6g	0%

Per cent daily values are based on a 2000 calorie diet

Honeyed Oranges ▶

APRICOT SORBET

SERVES 4

S orbets are always refreshing and this is no exception. Traditionally they are served part way through a meal to clear the palate, but are equally welcome at the end.

≈ Set the freezer to rapid freeze. Place the sugar and orange juice in a pan with 150 ml (¼ pint) water. Cook over gentle heat to dissolve. Add a further 300 ml (½ pint) water to the pan.
≈ Place the apricots in a food processor and purée for 30 seconds until smooth. Stir the apricot purée into the sugar syrup, place in a freezerproof container and freeze for 1 hour until half frozen. Whisk the egg white in a clean bowl until peaking and whisk in the sugar.

≈ Turn the half frozen fruit mixture into a bowl and whisk until smooth. Fold in the egg white and return to a freezerproof container. Freeze for 45 minutes.
≈ Turn the mixture out into a bowl, whisk again and return to a clean freezerproof container. Freeze for a further 2 hours until solid. Place the sorbet in the refrigerator 10 minutes before serving. Scoop into serving dishes, decorate and serve.

175 g (6 oz) sugar

juice of ½ orange

450 g (1 lb) apricots, stoned and chopped

1 egg white

30 g (2 tbsp) caster sugar

apricot slices, mint sprigs and orange zest to decorate

NUTRITION FACTS

Serving Size 1 (210g)

Calories 247	Calories from Fat 9
	% Daily Value
Total Fat 1g	1%
Saturated Fat 0g	0%
Monounsaturated Fat 0.2g	0%
Polyunsaturated Fat 0.1g	0%
Cholesterol 0mg	0%
Sodium 16mg	1%
Total Carbohydrate 61g	20%
Dietary Fibre 3g	13%
Sugars 56g	0%
Protein 3g	0%

Per cent daily values are based on a 2000 calorie diet

MELON ICE

SERVES 4

A ny melon is suitable for this recipe. Incredibly colourful and refreshing, it is the perfect light end to any meal.

≈ Set the freezer to rapid freeze. Place the sugar in a pan with 125 ml (4 fl oz) water. Add the mint and cook over a gentle heat until the sugar dissolves. Remove the pan from the heat and strain the syrup. Discard the mint sprigs. Stir in 300 ml (1½ pints) of cold water.
≈ Place the melon in a food processor and purée for 30 seconds until smooth. Stir into the syrup. Mix well and cool. Place the mixture in a freezerproof container and freeze for 1 hour.

≈ Remove from the freezer and pour the melon mixture into a bowl and whisk until smooth. Return to a clean freezer-proof container and freeze for a further 30 minutes. Repeat the whisking process every 30 minutes for 2½ hours. Scoop into dishes, decorate with mint, and serve immediately.

115 g (4 oz) sugar

3 mint sprigs

450 g (1 lb) melon, such as cantaloupe, galia or watermelon, seeded and diced

mint to decorate

NUTRITION FACTS

Serving Size 1 (149g)

Calories 137	Calories from Fat 0
	% Daily Value
Total Fat 0g	0%
Saturated Fat 0g	0%
Monounsaturated Fat 0.0g	0%
Polyunsaturated Fat 0.0g	0%
Cholesterol 0mg	0%
Sodium 25mg	1%
Total Carbohydrate 34g	12%
Dietary Fibre 1g	5%
Sugars 24g	0%
Protein 1g	0%

Per cent daily values are based on a 2000 calorie diet

Melon Ice ▶

FRUDITÉES

SERVES 4

*A sweet variation of "cruditées", this recipe is simple and easy to eat.
An informal dessert to be shared with friends.*

150 g (5 oz) strawberries, halved

1 green eating apple, cored and
sliced

2 bananas, cut into 2.5 cm (1 in)
chunks

1 kiwi fruit, cut into eight

10 ml (2 tsp) lemon juice

fresh mint to decorate

For the yogurt dip

250 ml (8 fl oz) low-fat natural yogurt

15 g (1 tbsp) soft brown sugar

dash of ground cinnamon

1 small papaya, seeded and diced

mint and cinnamon to decorate

NUTRITION FACTS	
Serving Size 1 (268g)	
Calories 162	Calories from Fat 18
	% Daily Value
Total Fat 2g	3%
Saturated Fat 1g	4%
Monounsaturated Fat 0.3g	0%
Polyunsaturated Fat 0.3g	0%
Cholesterol 3mg	1%
Sodium 44mg	2%
Total Carbohydrate 35g	12%
Dietary Fibre 5g	21%
Sugars 25g	0%
Protein 4g	0%

Per cent daily values are based on a 2000 calorie diet

≈ Prepare all the fruits. Sprinkle the apple and banana with the lemon juice.

≈ Place the yogurt dip ingredients in a food processor and liquidize for 30 seconds until smooth. Spoon into a serving bowl. Place the dip on a large serving plate, sprinkle with cinnamon, and arrange the fruit around. Serve with sprigs of mint.

BLUEBERRY CRUSH

SERVES 4

This is really quick to prepare, but requires freezing. Perfect to serve at a dinner party if you make it in advance.

≈ Place the meringues in a bowl. Add the blueberries and yogurt and mix well. Line a 750 ml (1¼ pint) pudding bowl with clingfilm and spoon in the mixture, pressing down well. Place in the freezer for 2 hours or until firm.

≈ Meanwhile for the sauce, place the blueberries, sugar and cranberry juice in a food processor. Liquidize for 30 seconds until smooth. Press through a sieve and chill until required.

≈ Dip the pudding bowl into hot water for 4 seconds. Invert the bowl onto a serving plate and unmould the pudding. Serve with the blueberry sauce.

150 g (5 oz) cooked meringue, broken into pieces
115 g (4 oz) blueberries
300 ml (1/2 pint) low-fat natural yogurt

For the sauce
115 g (4 oz) blueberries
30 g (2 tbsp) icing sugar
60 ml (4 tbsp) cranberry juice

NUTRITION FACTS	
Serving Size 1 (198g)	
Calories 216	Calories from Fat 9
	% Daily Value
Total Fat 1g	2%
Saturated Fat 1g	4%
Monounsaturated Fat 0.3g	0%
Polyunsaturated Fat 0.0g	0%
Cholesterol 4mg	1%
Sodium 97mg	4%
Total Carbohydrate 45g	15%
Dietary Fibre 2g	8%
Sugars 11g	0%
Protein 7g	0%

Per cent daily values are based on a 2000 calorie diet

APPLE CRUMBLE PIE

SERVES 8–12

A deep dish apple pie using filo or strudel pastry as the crust. Topped with a crumble mixture it is delicious served with natural yogurt.

≈ Lay a sheet of filo pastry in the base of a pie dish and up the sides. Brush lightly with melted margarine and continue layering pastry to cover the sides of the pie dish. Brush each sheet with margarine. Cook the pastry in the oven at 200°C (400°F, Gas 6) for 10 minutes.

≈ Meanwhile, place the apples, sugar, raisins and nutmeg in a pan. Cover and cook for 10 minutes or until the apples have softened. Mix together the topping ingredients.

≈ Spoon the apple filling into the pastry lined dish. Sprinkle on the topping, return to the oven and cook for 40 minutes until golden.

150 g (5 oz) filo pastry
25 g (1½ tbsp) polyunsaturated margarine, melted
900 g (2 lb) cooking apples, peeled and sliced
30 g (2 tbsp) soft brown sugar
30 g (2 tbsp) raisins
dash of grated nutmeg

For the topping
90 g (6 tbsp) plain flour
50 g (2 oz) porridge oats
50 g (2 oz) soft brown sugar
30 g (2 tbsp) polyunsaturated margarine

NUTRITION FACTS	
Serving Size 1 (161g)	
Calories 247	Calories from Fat 63
	% Daily Value
Total Fat 7g	11%
Saturated Fat 1g	11%
Monounsaturated Fat 2.5g	0%
Polyunsaturated Fat 2.3g	0%
Cholesterol 0mg	0%
Sodium 149mg	6%
Total Carbohydrate 45g	15%
Dietary Fibre 4g	16%
Sugars 11g	0%
Protein 3g	0%

Per cent daily values are based on a 2000 calorie diet

225 g (½ lb) bananas, chopped and
    frozen
15 ml (1 tbsp) lemon juice
90 g (6 tbsp) icing sugar
150 ml (¼ pint) low-fat natural yogurt
grated rind of 1 lemon
small meringues to serve (optional)

NUTRITION FACTS	
Serving Size 1 (115g)	
Calories 114	Calories from Fat 9
	% Daily Value
Total Fat 1g	1%
Saturated Fat 0g	2%
Monounsaturated Fat 0.2g	0%
Polyunsaturated Fat 0.0g	0%
Cholesterol 2mg	1%
Sodium 27mg	1%
Total Carbohydrate 32g	11%
Dietary Fibre 1g	6%
Sugars 20g	0%
Protein 3g	0%

Per cent daily values are based on a 2000 calorie diet

For the mousse
300 ml (½ pint) low-fat natural yogurt
150 ml (¼ pint) skimmed milk
    cheese or low-fat cream cheese
5 ml (1 tsp) vanilla extract
60 g (4 tbsp) vanilla sugar
15 ml (1 tbsp) brandy or sherry
15 g (1 tsp) vegetarian gelatine
2 large egg whites

For the sauce
300 g (1¾ cups) raspberries
juice of 1 orange
25 g (1 oz) icing sugar, sieved

NUTRITION FACTS	
Serving Size 1 (248g)	
Calories 373	Calories from Fat 9
	% Daily Value
Total Fat 1g	2%
Saturated Fat 1g	4%
Monounsaturated Fat 0.3g	0%
Polyunsaturated Fat 0.2g	0%
Cholesterol 4mg	1%
Sodium 82mg	3%
Total Carbohydrate 51g	17%
Dietary Fibre 3g	11%
Sugars 22g	0%
Protein 10g	0%

Per cent daily values are based on a 2000 calorie diet

BANANA ICE CREAM

SERVES 4

*This is really a cheat ice cream. Made with frozen bananas and natural yogurt,
the freezing time of the completed recipe is greatly reduced.*

≈ Set the freezer to rapid freeze. Place the frozen bananas in a food processor with the lemon juice, icing sugar and yogurt. Process for 1 minute or until smooth. Stir in the lemon rind.

≈ Place the mixture in a freezerproof container, cover and freeze for 2 hours or until set. Scoop into dishes and serve with small meringues.

VANILLA MOUSSE

SERVES 4

*This light and fluffy mousse tastes as good as it looks. Sliced and served with the
raspberry sauce it is a dieter's dream.*

≈ Place the yogurt, cheese, vanilla extract, sugar and alcohol in a food processor, liquidize for 30 seconds until smooth. Pour into a mixing bowl.
≈ Sprinkle the gelatine on to 60 ml (4 tablespoons) of cold water. Stir until dissolved and heat to boiling point. Boil for 2 minutes. Cool. Stir into the yogurt mixture. Whisk the egg whites until peaking and fold into the mousse.

≈ Line a 900 ml (1½ pint) loaf tin with clingfilm. Pour the mousse into the prepared tin and chill for 2 hours until set.
≈ Meanwhile, place the sauce ingredients in a food processor and liquidize until smooth. Press through a sieve to discard the seeds. Unmould the mousse on to a plate, remove the clingfilm, slice and serve with the sauce.

Vanilla Mousse ▶

BLUEBERRY CHEESECAKE

SERVES 6

A cheesecake with a delicious muesli and dried fig base, in place of the usual biscuits and butter, which gives a rich and crunchy base to the soft filling.

For the base

115 g (4 oz) muesli

150 g (5 oz) dried figs

For the filling

5 g (1 tsp) vegetarian gelatine

125 ml (4 fl oz) skimmed evaporated milk

1 egg

90 g (6 tbsp) caster sugar

450 g (1 lb) low-fat cottage cheese

50 g (2 oz) blueberries

For the topping

225 g (8 oz) blueberries

2 nectarines, pitted and sliced

30 ml (2 tbsp) honey

≈ Place the muesli and dried figs in a food processor and liquidize for 30 seconds. Press into the base of a base lined 20 cm (8 in) springform tin and chill while preparing the filling.

≈ Sprinkle the gelatine on to 60 ml (4 tablespoons) of cold water. Stir until dissolved and heat to boiling point. Boil for 2 minutes. Cool. Place the milk, egg, sugar and cheese in a food processor and liquidize until smooth. Stir in the blueberries. Place in a mixing bowl and gradually stir in the dissolved gelatine. Pour the mixture on to the base and chill for 2 hours until set.

≈ Remove the cheesecake from the pan and arrange the fruit for the topping in alternate rings on top. Drizzle the honey over the fruit and serve.

NUTRITION FACTS	
Serving Size 1 (238g)	
Calories 215	Calories from Fat 18
	% Daily Value
Total Fat 2g	3%
Saturated Fat 1g	4%
Monounsaturated Fat 0.6g	0%
Polyunsaturated Fat 0.2g	0%
Cholesterol 39mg	13%
Sodium 333mg	14%
Total Carbohydrate 40g	13%
Dietary Fibre 3g	13%
Sugars 44g	0%
Protein 13g	0%

Per cent daily values are based on a 2000 calorie diet

CRÈME CARAMEL

MAKES 4

Although low in fat, this recipe uses two whole eggs and should therefore follow a main course which does not use eggs to balance the fat content of the meal.

5 g (2 tsp) caster sugar

2 eggs, beaten

300 ml (½ pint) skimmed milk

2.5 ml (½ tsp) vanilla extract

dash of ground cinnamon

≈ Dissolve the 115 g (4 oz) sugar in a pan with 150 ml (¼ pint) cold water. Bring to the boil and boil rapidly until the mixture begins to turn golden brown. Pour into the base of 4 × 150 ml (¼ pint) ramekin dishes.

≈ Whisk the remaining sugar with the eggs in a bowl. Heat the milk with the vanilla and cinnamon until just boiling and gradually whisk into the egg mixture.

≈ Pour into the ramekins and place in a shallow roasting tin with enough hot water to reach halfway up the sides. Cover and cook in the oven at 180°C (350°F, Gas 4) for 50 minutes until set. Remove from the pan, slightly cool and chill in the refrigerator for 1 hour. Unmould on to individual plates and serve immediately.

Blueberry Cheesecake ▶

NUTRITION FACTS	
Serving Size 1 (130g)	
Calories 171	Calories from Fat 18
	% Daily Value
Total Fat 2g	4%
Saturated Fat 1g	4%
Monounsaturated Fat 1.0g	0%
Polyunsaturated Fat 0.3g	0%
Cholesterol 106mg	35%
Sodium 71mg	3%
Total Carbohydrate 32g	10%
Dietary Fibre 0g	0%
Sugars 30g	0%
Protein 6g	0%

Per cent daily values are based on a 2000 calorie diet

PLUM AND GINGER BRÛLÉE

SERVES 4

Plums and ginger are a great combination in this easy brûlée recipe, the ginger adding just enough spice to complement the plums.

4 plums, stoned and chopped

250 ml (8 fl oz) half-fat cream substitute

250 ml (8 fl oz) low-fat natural yogurt

2.5 g (½ tsp) ground ginger

60 g (4 tbsp) soft brown sugar

≈ Spoon the plums into the base of 4 × 150 ml (¼ pint) ramekin dishes. Lightly whip the cream substitute and fold in the yogurt and ground ginger. Spoon on to the fruit and chill for 2 hours.

≈ Sprinkle the brown sugar on top of the yogurt mixture and grill for 5 minutes or until the sugar has dissolved. Chill for 20 minutes before serving.

NUTRITION FACTS

Serving Size 1 (479g)

Calories 344	Calories from Fat 27

	% Daily Value
Total Fat 3g	4%
Saturated Fat 1g	4%
Monounsaturated Fat 1.4g	0%
Polyunsaturated Fat 0.4g	0%
Cholesterol 4mg	1%
Sodium 86mg	4%
Total Carbohydrate 74g	25%
Dietary Fibre 4g	14%
Sugars 46g	0%
Protein 8g	0%

Per cent daily values are based on a 2000 calorie diet

CAPPUCCINO SPONGES

SERVES 4

These individual sponge puddings are delicious served with the low-fat coffee sauce. Ideal for dinner parties, they look more delicate and attractive than one large pudding.

30 g (2 tbsp) polyunsaturated margarine

30 g (2 tbsp) soft brown sugar

2 egg whites

50 g (2 oz) plain flour

4 g (¾ tsp) baking powder

90 ml (6 tbsp) skimmed milk

5 ml (1 tsp) coffee extract

2.5 g (½ tsp) unsweetened cocoa powder

For the coffee sauce

300 ml (½ pint) skimmed milk

15 g (1 tbsp) soft brown sugar

5 ml (1 tsp) coffee extract

5 ml (1 tsp) coffee liqueur (optional)

30 g (2 tbsp) cornflour

≈ Use non-stick spray to lightly grease 4 × 150 ml (¼ pint) individual pudding moulds. Cream the margarine and the sugar together in a bowl and add the egg whites. Sieve the flour and baking powder together and fold into the creamed mixture with a metal spoon. Gradually stir in the milk, coffee extract and cocoa.

≈ Spoon equal amounts of the mixture into the moulds. Cover with pleated greaseproof paper, then foil, and tie securely with string. Place in a steamer or pan with sufficient boiling water to reach halfway up the sides of the moulds. Cover and cook for 30 minutes or until cooked through.

≈ Meanwhile, place the milk, sugar, coffee extract and coffee liqueur in a pan to make the sauce. Blend the cornflour with 60 ml (4 tablespoons) of cold water and stir into the pan. Bring to the boil, stirring until thickened. Reduce the heat and cook for a further 2–3 minutes.

≈ Carefully remove the cooked puddings from the steamer. Remove the paper and foil and unmould on to individual plates. Spoon the sauce around and serve.

NUTRITION FACTS

Serving Size 1 (154g)

Calories 199	Calories from Fat 54

	% Daily Value
Total Fat 6g	9%
Saturated Fat 1g	6%
Monounsaturated Fat 2.6g	0%
Polyunsaturated Fat 1.9g	0%
Cholesterol 2mg	1%
Sodium 241mg	10%
Total Carbohydrate 29g	10%
Dietary Fibre 1g	2%
Sugars 12g	0%
Protein 7g	0%

Per cent daily values are based on a 2000 calorie diet

Plum and Ginger Brûlée ▶

CINNAMON TOASTS

SERVES 4

This recipe is based on the classic breakfast dish. Here cinnamon is added to the milk and egg mixture to give a warm, spicy flavour to the recipe.

4 thick slices white bread, crusts
    removed and halved diagonally

150 ml (¼ pint) skimmed milk

5 g (1 tsp) ground cinnamon

1 egg, beaten

2 oranges, peeled, halved and sliced

2 kiwi fruit, peeled, halved and thinly
    sliced

20 g (4 tsp) soft brown sugar

For the yogurt sauce

150 ml (¼ pint) low-fat natural yogurt

10 ml (2 tsp) honey

dash of ground cinnamon

cinnamon to sprinkle

NUTRITION FACTS	
Serving Size 1 (228g)	
Calories 198	Calories from Fat 27
	% Daily Value
Total Fat 3g	5%
Saturated Fat 1g	6%
Monounsaturated Fat 1.1g	0%
Polyunsaturated Fat 0.5g	0%
Cholesterol 56mg	18%
Sodium 195mg	8%
Total Carbohydrate 36g	12%
Dietary Fibre 4g	17%
Sugars 20g	0%
Protein 8g	0%

Per cent daily values are based on a 2000 calorie diet

≈ Arrange the bread in a shallow dish. Mix together the milk, cinnamon and egg and pour over the bread. Leave to stand for 30 minutes.

≈ Remove the bread from the dish and cook one side under the grill for 4–5 minutes. Turn the bread over and grill for 2 minutes.

≈ Arrange the fruit in alternate layers on top of the bread and sprinkle each with 5 g (1 teaspoon) of sugar. Grill for 3 minutes until the sugar begins to dissolve.

≈ Mix together the yogurt sauce ingredients, sprinkle with cinnamon, and serve with the hot cinnamon toasts.

BAKED APPLES

SERVES 4

*U*sually filled with a suet-based mincemeat mixture, baked apples are a wonderful winter dessert. In this recipe, dried fruits and sugar have been used as a low-fat alternative.

≈ Wash the apples, dry, and remove the cores. Mix together the raisins, apricots, mixed peel, dates, margarine, sugar and lemon zest. Spoon into the hollowed centres of the apples. Score the skin around the apple, approximately 2.5 cm (1 in) from the top.

≈ Stand the apples in an ovenproof dish and pour a little water around them. Bake in the oven at 180°C (350°F, Gas 4) for 45 minutes or until cooked.

≈ Meanwhile, mix together the yogurt, honey and lemon zest. Remove the apples from the dish and serve with the yogurt.

4 large cooking apples
45 g (3 tbsp) raisins
30 g (2 tbsp) dried apricots, finely chopped
45 g (3 tbsp) chopped mixed candied peel
40 g (1½ oz) stoned dried dates, finely chopped
15 g (1 tbsp) polyunsaturated margarine
30 g (2 tbsp) soft brown sugar
grated zest of 1 lemon

For the yogurt sauce
150 ml (¼ pint) low-fat natural yogurt
10 ml (2 tsp) honey
grated rind of ½ lemon

NUTRITION FACTS	
Serving Size 1 (219g)	
Calories 233	Calories from Fat 36
	% Daily Value
Total Fat 4g	6%
Saturated Fat 1g	5%
Monounsaturated Fat 1.4g	0%
Polyunsaturated Fat 1.1g	0%
Cholesterol 2mg	1%
Sodium 64mg	3%
Total Carbohydrate 50g	17%
Dietary Fibre 5g	18%
Sugars 43g	0%
Protein 3g	0%

Per cent daily values are based on a 2000 calorie diet

POACHED PEARS

SERVES 4

*T*hese whole pears are cooked in alcohol and sugar to give them a delicious flavour and colour. Serve with low-fat natural yogurt if preferred.

≈ Place the pears in a pan with the vermouth, 150 ml (¼ pint) water, the sugar and cassis. Heat gently to dissolve the sugar. Cover and cook for 10 minutes, basting occasionally.

≈ Stir in the blueberries and cook for a further 5 minutes. Transfer to a serving dish and chill until required.

4 ripe pears, peeled
150 ml (¼ pint) vermouth
30 g (2 tbsp) caster sugar
15 ml (1 tbsp) cassis
50 g (2 oz) blueberries

NUTRITION FACTS	
Serving Size 1 (198g)	
Calories 148	Calories from Fat 9
	% Daily Value
Total Fat 1g	1%
Saturated Fat 0g	0%
Monounsaturated Fat 0.1g	0%
Polyunsaturated Fat 0.2g	0%
Cholesterol 0mg	0%
Sodium 1mg	0%
Total Carbohydrate 35g	12%
Dietary Fibre 4g	18%
Sugars 25g	0%
Protein 1g	0%

Per cent daily values are based on a 2000 calorie diet

Favourite Cakes, Cookies and Breads

APPLE BRAN CAKE

SERVES 12

Chunks of apple add moisture to this filling cake. Decorate with apple slices just before serving or brush with a little lemon juice if wishing to store the cake.

≈ Grease and base line a deep 20 cm (8 in) round cake tin.

≈ Place the apple sauce in a mixing bowl with the sugar and milk. Sieve the flour into the bowl and add the bran, baking powder, cinnamon, honey and apples. Whisk the egg whites until peaking and fold into the mixture. Spoon the mixture into the prepared tin and level the surface.

≈ Bake in the oven at 300°C (150°F, Gas 2) for 1¼–1½ hours or until cooked through. Cool in the tin for 10 minutes, then turn on to a wire rack and cool completely. Arrange the apple slices on top and drizzle with honey.

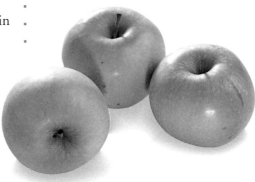

Ingredients

115 g (4 oz) plus 30 ml (2 tbsp) apple sauce

75 g (3 oz) plus 30 g (2 tbsp) brown sugar

45 ml (3 tbsp) skimmed milk

175 g (6 oz) plain flour

25 g (1 oz) all-bran cereal

10 g (2 tsp) baking powder

5 g (1 tsp) ground cinnamon

30 ml (2 tbsp) honey

150 g (5 oz) apples, peeled and chopped

2 egg whites

apple slices and 15 ml (1 tbsp) honey to decorate

NUTRITION FACTS	
Serving Size 1 (70g)	
Calories 137	Calories from Fat 0
	% Daily Value
Total Fat 0g	0%
Saturated Fat 0g	0%
Monounsaturated Fat 0.0g	0%
Polyunsaturated Fat 0.1g	0%
Cholesterol 0mg	0%
Sodium 120mg	5%
Total Carbohydrate 32g	11%
Dietary Fibre 2g	7%
Sugars 16g	0%
Protein 3g	0%

Per cent daily values are based on a 2000 calorie diet

FRUIT AND NUT LOAF

SERVES 12

This is a sweet fruity bread as opposed to a "tea" loaf. If liked, spread slices of the bread with a little polyunsaturated margarine to serve.

≈ Sieve the flour and salt into a bowl. Rub in the margarine, then stir in the sugar, raisins, walnuts and yeast. Place the milk in a pan with 75 ml (5 tablespoons) of water. Heat gently until lukewarm, but do not boil. Add the lukewarm liquid to the dry ingredients in the bowl and bring the mixture together to form a dough.

≈ Turn the dough onto a lightly floured surface and knead the dough for 5–7 minutes until smooth and elastic. Shape the dough into a round and place on a non-stick baking sheet. Make parallel diagonal slits across the top of the loaf, working from left to right. Then turn the knife and work back towards you making parallel diagonal slits to form "diamond" shapes. Cover and prove in a warm place for 1 hour or until doubled in size.

≈ Bake in the oven at 220°C (425°F, Gas 7) for 35 minutes or until cooked through. Place on a wire rack and brush with honey. Cool and serve.

Apple Bran Cake ▶

Ingredients

225 g (8 oz) white bread flour

2.5 g (½ tsp) salt

15 g (1 tbsp) polyunsaturated margarine

15 g (1 tbsp) caster sugar

75 g (3 oz) raisins

25 g (1 oz) walnuts, chopped

10 g (2 tsp) active dry yeast

75 ml (5 tbsp) skimmed milk

15 ml (1 tbsp) honey

NUTRITION FACTS	
Serving Size 1 (44g)	
Calories 139	Calories from Fat 18
	% Daily Value
Total Fat 2g	4%
Saturated Fat 0g	2%
Monounsaturated Fat 0.7g	0%
Polyunsaturated Fat 1.1g	0%
Cholesterol 0mg	0%
Sodium 113mg	5%
Total Carbohydrate 26g	9%
Dietary Fibre 1g	5%
Sugars 8g	0%
Protein 4g	0%

Per cent daily values are based on a 2000 calorie diet

ANGEL CAKE

SERVES 12

Although it sounds complicated, this recipe is very easy to make. Be sure to treat the mixture gently so as not to beat out all of the air.

3 eggs

90 g (6 tbsp) caster sugar

25 g (1 oz) self raising flour

few drops of pink food colouring

few drops of yellow food colouring

For the filling

225 g (8 oz) low-fat soft cheese, such as curd or cream cheese

30 g (2 tbsp) icing sugar

≈ Line 3 × 900 g (2 lb) loaf tins with non-stick baking paper. Whisk the eggs and sugar in a large bowl until thick and pale and the whisk leaves a trail in the mixture when lifted. Sieve the flour into the mixture and fold in gently.

≈ Divide the mixture into three equal quantities and place in separate bowls. Add a few drops of pink colouring to one bowl and stir in gently. Add a few drops of yellow food colouring to another bowl and stir in gently.

≈ Spoon the pink mixture into one prepared tin, the yellow into another and the plain mixture into the third. Bake in the oven at 200°C (400°F, Gas 6) for 10 minutes until the mixture springs back when gently pressed. Turn out and cool completely on a wire rack.

≈ Trim the sides from each cake. Mix together the filling ingredients. Place the yellow cake on a chopping board and spread half of the filling on top. Place the pink cake on top and spread with the remaining filling. Top with the white cake. Dust with icing sugar and slice to serve.

NUTRITION FACTS	
Serving Size 1 (28g)	
Calories 74	Calories from Fat 9
	% Daily Value
Total Fat 1g	2%
Saturated Fat 0g	2%
Monounsaturated Fat 0.5g	0%
Polyunsaturated Fat 0.2g	0%
Cholesterol 53mg	18%
Sodium 115mg	5%
Total Carbohydrate 13g	4%
Dietary Fibre 0g	1%
Sugars 7g	0%
Protein 2g	0%

Per cent daily values are based on a 2000 calorie diet

GINGERBREAD

SERVES 16

Skimmed milk, prunes and egg white are used in this classic cake to reduce the fat content. For an extra spicy flavour, add 15 g (1 teaspoon) of ground allspice to the mixture as well as the ginger.

450 g (1 lb) plain flour

dash of salt

15 g (1 tbsp) ground ginger

15 g (1 tbsp) baking powder

5 ml (1 tsp) bicarbonate of soda

175 g (6 oz) soft brown sugar

185 g (6½ oz) molasses

150 ml (5 fl oz) golden syrup

115 g (4 oz) dried stoned prunes

300 ml (½ pint) skimmed milk

1 egg white

icing sugar for dusting

2 pieces stem ginger, chopped

≈ Grease and line a 23 cm (9 in) square tin. Sift the flour, salt, ground ginger, baking powder and soda into a large bowl.

≈ Place the sugar, molasses and syrup in a pan and heat gently to dissolve. Place the prunes in a food processor with 45 ml (3 tablespoons) of water and liquidize for 30 seconds until puréed. Add the milk to the sugar mixture and stir into the dry ingredients with the prunes. Whisk the egg white until peaking, fold into the mixture and spoon into the prepared tin.

≈ Bake in the oven at 160°C (325°F, Gas 3) for 55 minutes–1 hour or until firm. Cool in the pan for 10 minutes. Turn the cake out on to a wire rack and cool completely. Cut into 16 pieces. Dust with icing sugar and top with chopped ginger.

NUTRITION FACTS	
Serving Size 1 (107g)	
Calories 267	Calories from Fat 0
	% Daily Value
Total Fat 0g	1%
Saturated Fat 0g	0%
Monounsaturated Fat 0.0g	0%
Polyunsaturated Fat 0.1g	0%
Cholesterol 0mg	0%
Sodium 231mg	10%
Total Carbohydrate 62g	21%
Dietary Fibre 2g	6%
Sugars 23g	0%
Protein 4g	0%

Per cent daily values are based on a 2000 calorie diet

Gingerbread ▶

OAT AND ORANGE COOKIES

MAKES 20

These little cookies are hard to resist. Rolled in oats, they have a crunchy outside, and softer inside which has a mild orange flavour.

45 g (3 tbsp) polyunsaturated
   margarine
40 g (1½ oz) soft brown sugar
1 egg white, lightly beaten
30 ml (2 tbsp) skimmed milk
45 g (3 tbsp) raisins
grated zest of 1 orange
150 g (5 oz) self raising flour
40 g (1½ oz) porridge oats
strips of orange zest to decorate
   (optional)

NUTRITION FACTS	
Serving Size 1 (20g)	
Calories 69	Calories from Fat 18
	% Daily Value
Total Fat 2g	3%
Saturated Fat 0g	2%
Monounsaturated Fat 0.8g	0%
Polyunsaturated Fat 0.6g	0%
Cholesterol 0mg	0%
Sodium 124mg	5%
Total Carbohydrate 12g	4%
Dietary Fibre 1g	2%
Sugars 4g	0%
Protein 1g	0%

Per cent daily values are based on a 2000 calorie diet

≈ Cream the margarine and sugar together until light and fluffy. Add the egg white, milk, raisins and orange zest. Fold in the flour and bring the mixture together to form a dough. Roll into 20 equal-sized balls.

≈ Place the oats in a shallow bowl, roll each dough ball in the oats to coat completely, pressing them on gently. Place the cookies on non-stick baking sheets, spacing well apart. Flatten each round slightly.

≈ Bake in the oven at 180°C (350°F, Gas 4) for 15 minutes or until golden. Cool on a wire rack, decorate and store any leftovers in an airtight container.

RAISIN AND HONEY BREAD

SERVES 16

This loaf contains a high proportion of yogurt which gives it a white, light centre.

≈ Mix the flour, baking powder, bicarbonate of soda and salt in a large bowl. Whisk together the yogurt and egg whites and fold into the flour mixture with the raisins and honey.

≈ Grease a 900 g (2 lb) loaf tin and spoon in the mixture. Bake in the oven at 220°C (425°F, Gas 7) for 20 minutes until golden. Cool slightly and turn out of the pan. Serve warm.

250 g (9 oz) plain flour

7.5 g (1½ tsp) baking powder

2.5 g (½ tsp) bicarbonate of soda

2.5 g (½ tsp) salt

425 ml (14 fl oz) low-fat natural yogurt

2 egg whites

40 g (1½ oz) raisins

30 ml (2 tbsp) honey

polyunsaturated margarine for greasing

NUTRITION FACTS	
Serving Size 1 (53g)	
Calories 102	Calories from Fat 9
	% Daily Value
Total Fat 1g	1%
Saturated Fat 0g	2%
Monounsaturated Fat 0.2g	0%
Polyunsaturated Fat 0.1g	0%
Cholesterol 2mg	1%
Sodium 141mg	6%
Total Carbohydrate 20g	7%
Dietary Fibre 1g	2%
Sugars 6g	0%
Protein 4g	0%

Per cent daily values are based on a 2000 calorie diet

115 g (4 oz) stoned dried prunes

115 g (4 oz) soft brown sugar

45 g (3 tbsp) unsweetened cocoa
  powder, sieved

50 g (2 oz) plain flour

5 g (1 tsp) baking powder

3 egg whites

icing sugar for dusting

NUTRITION FACTS

Serving Size 1 (36g)	
Calories 90	Calories from Fat 0

	% Daily Value
Total Fat 0g	0%
Saturated Fat 0g	0%
Monounsaturated Fat 0.0g	0%
Polyunsaturated Fat 0.0g	0%
Cholesterol 0mg	0%
Sodium 45mg	2%
Total Carbohydrate 22g	7%
Dietary Fibre 1g	3%
Sugars 17g	0%
Protein 1g	0%

Per cent daily values are based on a 2000 calorie diet

CHOCOLATE BROWNIES

MAKES 16

Chocolate brownies in a low-fat book? They taste just as good as the real thing but have a slightly different texture. Keep in an airtight container if you can resist them for long enough.

≈ Grease and line a shallow 18 cm (7 in) square cake tin.

≈ Place the prunes in a food processor with 45 ml (3 tablespoons) of water and liquidize to a purée. Transfer the purée to a mixing bowl and stir in the sugar, cocoa, flour and baking powder. Whisk the egg whites until peaking and fold into the mixture. Pour into the prepared tin and level the surface.

≈ Bake in the oven at 180°C (350°F, Gas 4) for 1 hour or until cooked through. Let the brownies cool in the tin for 10 minutes, then turn out on to a wire rack and cool completely. Cut into 16 squares, dust with icing sugar and serve.

---

1 packet active dry yeast

450 g (1 lb) wholemeal flour

10 g (2 tsp) caster sugar

10 g (2 tsp) salt

30 g (2 tbsp) polyunsaturated
  margarine

10 g (2 tsp) caraway seeds

10 g (2 tsp) fennel seeds

10 g (2 tsp) sesame seeds

1 egg white

NUTRITION FACTS

Serving Size 1 (48g)	
Calories 161	Calories from Fat 27

	% Daily Value
Total Fat 3g	5%
Saturated Fat 1g	3%
Monounsaturated Fat 1.0g	0%
Polyunsaturated Fat 0.9g	0%
Cholesterol 0mg	0%
Sodium 418mg	17%
Total Carbohydrate 30g	10%
Dietary Fibre 5g	21%
Sugars 1g	0%
Protein 6g	0%

Per cent daily values are based on a 2000 calorie diet

SEED BREAD

SERVES 12

The seeds in this loaf add flavour and texture to the bread. Easy to eat, it is divided into six portions which are simply broken off for serving.

≈ Place the yeast, flour, sugar and salt in a large bowl. Rub in the margarine and add half of each of the seeds. Stir in 300 ml (½ pint) tepid water and mix well. Bring the mixture together to form a soft dough. Knead the dough for 5 minutes on a lightly floured surface and break into six equal pieces.

≈ Lightly grease a deep 15 cm (6 in) round cake tin. Shape each of the dough pieces into a round. Place five pieces around the edge of the tin and one in the centre. Cover and leave to prove in a warm place for 1 hour or until doubled in size.

≈ Whisk the egg white and brush over the top of the dough. Sprinkle the remaining seeds on to the top of the dough, alternating the different types on each section of the loaf.

≈ Bake in the oven at 200°C (400°F, Gas 6) for 30 minutes or until cooked through. The loaf should sound hollow when tapped on the base. Cool slightly and serve.

Seed Bread ▶

HERBED CHEESE LOAF

SERVES 8

This loaf is best served warm straight from the oven to obtain the full flavour of the herbs and cheese.

1 packet active dry yeast

675 g (1½ lb) white bread flour

5 g (1 tsp) salt

5 g (1 tsp) caster sugar

15 g (½ oz) polyunsaturated
   margarine

45 g (3 tbsp) fresh chopped parsley

75 g (3 oz) low-fat cheese, grated

1 egg white

NUTRITION FACTS

Serving Size 1 (98g)

Calories 336	Calories from Fat 27
	% Daily Value
Total Fat 3g	5%
Saturated Fat 1g	3%
Monounsaturated Fat 0.8g	0%
Polyunsaturated Fat 1.0g	0%
Cholesterol 1mg	0%
Sodium 327mg	14%
Total Carbohydrate 63g	21%
Dietary Fibre 3g	10%
Sugars 1g	0%
Protein 12g	0%

Per cent daily values are based on a 2000 calorie diet

≈ Place the yeast, flour, salt and sugar in a large mixing bowl. Rub in the margarine. Add the herbs and cheese and stir in 475 ml (16 fl oz) tepid water. Bring together to form a soft dough. Knead on a floured surface for 5–7 minutes until smooth.

≈ Divide the mixture into three equal portions. Roll each into a 35 cm (14 in) sausage shape. Place the dough pieces side by side and cross over each other at the top, pressing together to seal. Continue working down the length of the dough, crossing alternate strands to form a plait. Seal the end by pressing together and fold both ends under the plait.

≈ Place the bread on a non-stick baking sheet, cover and leave in a warm place for 1 hour or until doubled in size.

≈ Lightly beat the egg white and brush over the loaf. Bake in the oven at 200°C (400°F, Gas 6) for 30 minutes or until cooked through. The loaf will sound hollow when tapped. Serve.

WHOLEMEAL SODA BREAD

SERVES 12

This yeast-free bread is based on an Irish recipe where it is traditionally served. Made with wholemeal flour for extra goodness, it is filling and ideal served with soups.

175 g (6 oz) plain flour

175 g (6 oz) wholemeal flour

10 g (2 tsp) bicarbonate of soda

10 g (2 tsp) cream of tartar

2.5 g (½ tsp) salt

30 g (2 tbsp) polyunsaturated
   margarine

350 ml (12 fl oz) skimmed milk

2 egg whites

NUTRITION FACTS

Serving Size 1 (71g)

Calories 139	Calories from Fat 18
	% Daily Value
Total Fat 2g	4%
Saturated Fat 0g	2%
Monounsaturated Fat 0.9g	0%
Polyunsaturated Fat 0.8g	0%
Cholesterol 1mg	0%
Sodium 355mg	15%
Total Carbohydrate 25g	8%
Dietary Fibre 2g	9%
Sugars 2g	0%
Protein 5g	0%

Per cent daily values are based on a 2000 calorie diet

≈ Lightly grease and flour a baking sheet. Sieve the flours, bicarbonate of soda, cream of tartar and salt into a bowl. Add the contents of the sieve to the bowl.

≈ Rub in the margarine and gradually mix in the milk and beaten egg whites to form a dough. Shape the mixture into a round on a lightly floured surface. Score into four triangles with a knife and place on the prepared baking sheet. Bake in the oven at 220°C (425°F, Gas 7) for 30 minutes or until cooked. Serve warm.

Wholemeal Soda Bread ▶

PEAR UPSIDE-DOWN CAKE

SERVES 8

In this recipe, sliced pears are set on a caramel base and topped with a spicy sponge mixture. Once cooked, turn out and serve immediately with natural yogurt.

30 ml (2 tbsp) honey

30 g (2 tbsp) soft brown sugar

2 large pears, peeled, cored and sliced

60 g (4 tbsp) polyunsaturated margarine

50 g (2 oz) caster sugar

3 egg whites

115 g (4 oz) self raising flour

10 g (2 tsp) ground allspice

≈ Heat the honey and sugar in a pan until melted. Pour into a base lined 20 cm (8 in) round cake tin. Arrange the pears around the base of the tin.

≈ Cream the margarine and sugar together until light and fluffy. Whisk the egg whites until peaking and fold into the mixture with the flour and allspice. Spoon on top of the pears.

≈ Bake in the oven at 180°C (350°F, Gas 4) for 50 minutes or until risen and golden. Stand for 5 minutes, then turn out on to a serving plate. Remove the lining paper and serve.

≈ Decorate with walnuts, but remember that nuts are high in fat and are best saved for special occasions.

NUTRITION FACTS

Serving Size 1 (92g)

Calories 190	Calories from Fat 54

	% Daily Value
Total Fat 6g	9%
Saturated Fat 1g	6%
Monounsaturated Fat 2.6g	0%
Polyunsaturated Fat 1.9g	0%
Cholesterol 0mg	0%
Sodium 287mg	12%
Total Carbohydrate 32g	11%
Dietary Fibre 2g	6%
Sugars 18g	0%
Protein 3g	0%

Per cent daily values are based on a 2000 calorie diet

ROCKY MOUNTAIN BUNS

MAKES 12

There is a hint of coffee in these fun-to-eat small buns. The marshmallows and sultanas give them a "rocky," uneven appearance.

275 g (10 oz) self raising flour

2.5 g (½ tsp) salt

50 g (2 oz) polyunsaturated margarine

30 g (2 tbsp) caster sugar

45 g (3 tbsp) sultanas

25 g (1 oz) mini marshmallows

150 ml (¼ pint) skimmed milk

15 ml (1 tbsp) coffee extract

icing sugar for dusting

≈ Sieve the flour and salt into a bowl. Rub in the margarine until the mixture resembles breadcrumbs. Stir in the sugar, sultanas and marshmallows.

≈ Mix together the milk and coffee extract and stir into the mixture to form a soft dough. Place 12 equal-sized spoonfuls of mixture on a non-stick baking sheet, spacing slightly apart.

≈ Bake in the oven at 220°C (425°F, Gas 7) for 20 minutes until risen and golden. Cool on a wire rack and serve.

NUTRITION FACTS

Serving Size 1 (58g)

Calories 172	Calories from Fat 36

	% Daily Value
Total Fat 4g	6%
Saturated Fat 1g	4%
Monounsaturated Fat 1.7g	0%
Polyunsaturated Fat 1.3g	0%
Cholesterol 0mg	0%
Sodium 481mg	20%
Total Carbohydrate 30g	10%
Dietary Fibre 1g	4%
Sugars 10g	0%
Protein 3g	0%

Per cent daily values are based on a 2000 calorie diet

Pear Upside-down Cake ▶

175 g (6 oz) dried apricots, chopped

60 ml (4 tbsp) unsweetened orange juice

90 g (6 tbsp) polyunsaturated margarine, melted

60 ml (4 tbsp) honey

75 g (3 oz) semolina

115 g (4 oz) plus 30 g (2 tbsp) plain flour

NUTRITION FACTS

Serving Size 1 (95g)

Calories 223	Calories from Fat 54
	% Daily Value
Total Fat 6g	9%
Saturated Fat 1g	6%
Monounsaturated Fat 2.6g	0%
Polyunsaturated Fat 1.9g	0%
Cholesterol 0mg	0%
Sodium 69mg	3%
Total Carbohydrate 40g	13%
Dietary Fibre 2g	9%
Sugars 17g	0%
Protein 4g	0%

Per cent daily values are based on a 2000 calorie diet

APRICOT BARS

MAKES 8

These are very filling, healthy fruit bars. A delicious apricot purée is sandwiched between a shortcake mixture.

≈ Lightly grease an 18 cm (7 in) square cake tin. Place the apricots in a pan with the orange juice and simmer for 5 minutes. Drain if the juice has not been absorbed by the fruit.

≈ Heat the margarine and honey in a pan until melted. Add the semolina and flour and mix well. Press half of the semolina mixture into the base of the prepared tin. Spoon on the fruit mixture and top with the remaining semolina mixture, covering the fruit completely.

≈ Bake in the oven at 190°C (375°F, Gas 5) for 35 minutes until golden. Cool for 5 minutes in the tin, then cut into eight bars. Remove from the tin and cool completely.

50 g (2 oz) polyunsaturated margarine

250 g (9 oz) soft brown sugar

2 egg whites

150 g (5 oz) plain flour

45 g (3 tbsp) unsweetened cocoa powder, sifted

1.5 g (¼ tsp) bicarbonate of soda

1.5 g (¼ tsp) baking powder

250 ml (8 fl oz) skimmed milk

icing sugar and cocoa for dusting

NUTRITION FACTS

Serving Size 1 (75g)

Calories 195	Calories from Fat 36
	% Daily Value
Total Fat 4g	6%
Saturated Fat 1g	4%
Monounsaturated Fat 1.7g	0%
Polyunsaturated Fat 1.2g	0%
Cholesterol 0mg	0%
Sodium 102mg	4%
Total Carbohydrate 38g	13%
Dietary Fibre 0g	1%
Sugars 26g	0%
Protein 3g	0%

Per cent daily values are based on a 2000 calorie diet

LOW-FAT CHOCOLATE CAKE

SERVES 12

This chocolate cake is very rich and a small slice will satisfy any chocoholic for a while.

≈ Grease and flour a 20 cm (8 in) round cake tin. Cream the margarine and sugar in a bowl until light and fluffy. Add the egg whites and whisk into the mixture until thick.

≈ Place the flour, cocoa, bicarbonate of soda, and baking powder in a separate bowl. Add the milk gradually to the egg white mixture, alternating with the dry ingredients. Pour the mixture into the prepared tin.

≈ Bake in the oven at 180°C (350°F, Gas 4) for 1 hour or until cooked through. Allow to cool completely in the tin. Turn out and dust with the icing sugar and cocoa. Serve.

Apricot Bars ▶

124

CARROT AND PRUNE CAKE

SERVES 12

This recipe is traditionally high in fat, but this version uses prunes instead and only uses the whites of the eggs. Take extra care folding in the egg whites as a heavy hand will result in a heavy cake.

225 g (8 oz) carrots

425 g (15 oz) can prunes in fruit juice

40 g (1½ oz) soft brown sugar

275 g (10 oz) self raising flour

grated zest of 1 orange

45 g (3 tbsp) semolina

3 egg whites

For the icing

175 g (6 oz) low-fat soft cheese

15 g (1 tbsp) icing sugar, sieved

ground cinnamon and orange zest
    to decorate

NUTRITION FACTS	
Serving Size 1 (114g)	
Calories 228	Calories from Fat 0
	% Daily Value
Total Fat 0g	1%
Saturated Fat 0g	0%
Monounsaturated Fat 0.0g	0%
Polyunsaturated Fat 0.1g	0%
Cholesterol 0mg	0%
Sodium 360mg	15%
Total Carbohydrate 53g	18%
Dietary Fibre 2g	8%
Sugars 28g	0%
Protein 4g	0%

Per cent daily values are based on a 2000 calorie diet

≈ Grease and base line a 20 cm (8 in) deep cake tin. Grate the carrots and place in a bowl. Drain the prunes and discard the juice and stones. Liquidize the prunes in a food processor for 30 seconds and add to the carrot with the sugar.

≈ Add the flour, orange zest and semolina to the mixture, stirring well. Whisk the egg whites until peaks form and fold into the mixture. Spoon into the prepared tin and level the surface.

≈ Bake in the oven at 190°C (375°F, Gas 5) for 45 minutes or until cooked through. Cool in the pan for 10 minutes, turn out and cool completely on a wire rack.

≈ Mix together the cream cheese and icing sugar for the icing. Spread on top of the cake. Decorate and serve.

INDEX